Translated from the German by Helga Schier

Editor: Michael Part

This is a work of fiction. All names and characters
are either invented or used fictitiously.

Original title: Die Wilden Fussballkerle. Vanessa, Die Unerschrockene.
Baumhaus Verlag in the Bastei Luebbe Gmbh & Co. KG
© 2010 by Bastei Luebbe GmbH & Co. KG, Cologne
"Die Wilden Fußballkerle"™ und © dreammotion GmbH

Special thanks to:
Yonatan, Yaron, and Guy Ginsberg

Library of Congress Cataloging-in-Publication data in file.

ISBN 978-0-9844257-47

Published by Sole Books

First Edition December 2011
Printed in the United States of America

Layout: Lynn M. Snyder

10987654321

RMA578DR268, November, 2011

JOACHIM MASANNEK

The Wild Soccer Bunch

Hi *Wild Soccer Bunch* fans!

I'm so glad that you're reading the third book of the *Wild Soccer Bunch* series. This book is especially exciting because the hero is a girl. As we know from the U.S. Women's soccer team, which is one of the best teams in the world, girls are great at soccer!

All of us love playing soccer because it's fun! Although I'm a pro, which means I make a living being a soccer player, I get excited playing every single game as if it were my first. Each game is like an open book, and I always wonder what kind of story will unfold in the next 90 minutes.

Sometimes, the result of the game can be disappointing, but don't let losses stop you from playing the game you love. One thing you should always remember: Skill isn't the only thing you need in order to win. You need heart. And if you and your teammates are playing with a lot of heart, you can win while having the time of your life out on the field!

Enjoy the book, and have a great soccer season!

Your Friend and Teammate,

Landon Donovan

JOACHIM MASANNEK

The Wild Soccer Bunch

Book 3

Zoe the Fearless

Illustrations by Jan Birck

Sole
BOOKS

TABLE OF CONTENTS

I'm Losing It!

Hi! It's me, Zoe, and I'm real sorry, but there's a game going on and I can't talk. Shoot, Amelia! Why don't you just give the ball to the other side? Unbelievable!
This girl is too much! Amelia Dessert – and believe me, her game fits her name. The girl plays like a pile of soggy whipped cream. She just sits there! Okay, that was mean, but look, I'm just trying to play a real game of soccer here and these girls are just not cutting it.

I was playing at top speed, but that didn't seem to help one bit. The *Brookline Soccer Sirens* were in possession of the ball and charging our goal. Yes, yes, I know – *Soccer Sirens* – cute name, but who said soccer was cute? This is the kind of thing you have to put up with if you're stuck on a girls' soccer team. Our team name is no better: *Somerville Soccer Swallows* – and as much as it hurts, it fits. Flitting around the field like a bunch of little birds, making a breeze with our wings, and definitely not getting the job done. Actually, I'm talking about the other girls, not me. I'd been sitting in the grass, pouting, since about three minutes into the game. Ms. Squeamish, our coach, took me off the field because I got angry. And that's why Amelia was fluttering all over the field instead of me, and well, the rest is history.

The *Brookline Soccer Sirens* attacked. Their three forwards charged in perfect formation. Although the gals knew what it meant to play a position – and believe me, that's more than can be said of most of the other *girl* teams – there was no guarantee they'd actually pass the ball. Stubborn like a herd of cranky mares, my grandma would say, and I'm telling you, she knows what she's talking about.

"Come on! Attack! She'll never pass the ball!" I yelled at our defenders, ignoring the scowl on Coach Squeamish's face.

As usual, my darling teammates ignored me. Like good little girls, they did what we had practiced in training, and it was straight out of the book. What they *didn't* do was expect the unexpected. Instead, they covered the two other players, leaving the third alone with the ball. I'm sure they thought she'd pass it. Their jaws dropped when, as *I* expected, she *didn't* pass and plunked the ball right into the goal instead.

Nine zip for Brookline. That was it for me. I leaped up, balled my hands into fists, took a deep breath and... that's as far as I got.

"Zoe!" Coach Squeamish warned me. "One more word out of you and you'll *never* get back out on that field!"

I threw her one of my killer glances, but kept my mouth shut. I wanted to play – at any cost. Because at that moment our team bus arrived on the other end of the field. As usual, the boys' team of our soccer club had destroyed their opponents. They were the best of the best of all the U-10 teams in three counties. They were so good they had even tied Boston and Cambridge once.

Those boys were awesome! Don't get the wrong idea here. I'm eight years old, you know, and at my age girls couldn't care less about boys. Totally true. I know my grandma says different, but then again, my grandma has a thing about turning me into a beautiful young princess. Yech! Don't worry, she says, someday you'll change. I say, no way. That's what you call a real fairy tale.

Anyway, these boys were beyond awesome and as a team, they were the greatest. And all I wanted was to be one of them. Not a *boy*, you understand, but me, a girl, playing on their team, because I was good enough.

For two whole years I dreamed about just that, and on a Saturday like this one, I thought I had a chance to make my dream come true; on a Saturday like this one I could show them how good a player I really was. And then maybe, just maybe, they'd let go of their dumb ideas about not allowing girls on a boys' team. Maybe they'd see how great I played and ask me to join their team.

But Coach Squeamish didn't even *think* about putting me back in. Instead, the *Brookline Soccer Sirens* had an even bigger lead: thirteen-zero. The boys on the other end of the field roared with laughter. They made fun of us and mimicked Amelia as she huffed and puffed and wobbled after the ball. Then, at seventeen-zero, three minutes before the end of the game, Coach Squeamish finally showed me some mercy. "Okay, Zoe. Get in there. Play forward with Amelia. But I'm warning you, one bad word out of you and you are out of there!"

"No worries, Coach Squeamish!" I shouted and jumped up. "I won't tell her that she just sits there like a pile of whipped cream."

Coach Squeamish gasped, but I was long gone. I had already moved on to my next problem. The boys on the other side of the field whistled with excitement when I ran onto the field.

"Wow! Will you look at that!" they shouted. "They're

bringing in a substitute!"

"For the last three minutes of the game!"

"Guess she's going to save the game!"

The boys laughed loud and long and I could hear them laughing over the cheering crowd, and I could feel my face turn as red as a Ferrari, but that wasn't going to stop me. Those blockheads were going to get their money's worth!

I ran off, straight towards Amelia, who, wobbling and huffing and puffing, tried to keep up with the ball. I took the ball off her feet and stormed towards the Brookline goal. The *Soccer Sirens* came at me one by one, but I zigzagged through them like they were slalom poles. I left them all in the dust, and then I pulled the trigger and aimed directly into the corner. This being the first ever test for the Brookline goalie, she failed miserably and fell into the dirt. Coach Squeamish jumped up and down like a jack-in-the-box, shouting "Goal! Goal! Goal!"

But did that make me happy? No way. I was focused. And livid. It was seventeen to one, and there was only one reason for that: I had been benched. But the game was not over yet. I had two minutes to do some damage. That's why I jumped over the Brookline goalie, grabbed the ball and ran back to the kick-off point.

Kick-off was the only time the *Sirens* ever touched the ball. As soon as the referee blew his whistle, I tore free with the ball, brushed away the center forward and charged towards the goal. Twenty seconds later it was seventeen to two. Then seventeen to three! And as soon as I got in the groove, the referee called time and just as quickly as I had appeared, the game was over. I lived the dream for only a few minutes, but it was bound to be enough to impress the boys.

I shot a look their way, to see the amazement in their faces. I wanted to see them finally realize that I was good enough to be one of them. I couldn't wait to see that look on all their faces. Instead, I was crushed. I felt as if I had just been thrown into a bathtub full of ice cubes. The boys were gone. They had left. Just like that. I wasn't even important enough for them to stay and see my game. I was trembling with disappointment and anger. And while my teammates squeaked their appreciation to the *Brookline Soccer Sirens* despite our grim defeat, I shouldered my bag, pulled my hoodie over my long red hair, and split for the bike racks, never looking back.

There it was waiting for me, chained to the first bike rack, my most prized possession besides my soccer gear: a real Mongoose mountain bike, black as midnight, rear tire fatter than the front, and ready for some real BMX action. I knew my spirits would be up just as soon as I felt the wind in my hair. Of course, I still wished I could play on a real soccer team, but that didn't seem to be in the cards yet. I bent down, grabbed my lock, and turned it to the right number combination: my mom's birthday. And that got me to thinking about her. She died exactly fifty-two and a half weeks ago. I didn't have to think for long because that's when someone from behind me spoke up: "That is the coolest bike in the whole club!"

I turned around and there was Alex, the captain of the legendary youth soccer club, standing right in front of me. I tried to say something, but my mouth didn't work and I forgot how to talk. Alex grinned, and at first I thought he was laughing at me. But actually, he was

flustered too.

"This is going to sound weird but... we were watching your moves out there. Would uh, would you want to come to one of our practices some time?"

I was speechless, frozen in time. I couldn't even nod.

"I know we weren't exactly nice to you out there, so I don't blame you for not wanting to talk to me," Alex said.

I was about to explode. Finally, I found my voice. "But girls aren't supposed to play on boys' teams, right?" Then I thought about it. "Oh wait, I get it. You're inviting me to *watch* you practice," I said, disappointed.

"No," Alex said matter-of-factly. "I'm inviting you to play."

"But – how?" I shot back.

"We can have anybody we want on our team," Alex said, "Sure, all the teams are just boys' teams and girls' teams, but there's no rule that says every kid on my team has to be a boy. We want the best players on our team. We want you," Alex explained.

I couldn't believe what he was saying. I think I might have mouthed a word, but it didn't come out right and Alex just grinned. He wasn't that much older than me, but he seemed a whole lot wiser.

"Think about it," he said. "And if you decide you want to give it a shot, hop on this really cool bike of yours and see if it can find us."

He looked at me expectantly and I tell you, I wanted to hug him right then and there, I was so happy. But instead, I hopped on my bike and rode off and he shouted after me:

"Field three! Five to six thirty! Did you hear me?" I heard him and waved back. I heard him crystal clear. He was telling me I'd made it. After two long years of torture and gruesome humiliation with the *Somerville Swallows,* I'd finally get to play on a boys' team. I pounded my pedals. I was stronger than ever. This was the first step on the way to my greatest dream. I, Zoe Burns, would be the first woman ever to play on a U.S. Men's National Soccer Team. Impossible, you say? Watch me.

That morning I was sure my dreams would come true. I raced over the fields and crossed the dam, and I didn't stop until I could see the ocean and I kept on going until I could hear it and taste it. I screamed my joy to the wind: what a glorious day! And tomorrow was going to be even better, because it was my ninth birthday!

NO!

The car door closed quietly with an expensive thud. If you guessed fancy, you'd be right, a very fancy Cadillac. If you guessed the thud was anything but a thud, you'd be wrong. This thud was the worst sound I had ever heard in my entire life. This was the thud that *destroyed* my life. It was as if my life was blown up with one finger.

Then all was still. Still and quiet. But inside me, anger and desperation were having a shouting match so loud I had to cover my ears. "NO!" they screamed incessantly.

But nobody listened.

I sat in the passenger seat, my face resting against the cold window. I sat there, watching my own funeral. Talk about a nightmare. You've heard of the movie "Nightmare on Elm Street"? This was the nightmare on *my* street.

The car quivered slightly when my father started the engine. Then we drove off. Silently, as if I had left my body, I floated along the street I had lived on my entire life, all 3,285 days of it. Silently, I floated out of town. I felt nothing except my father's eyes staring at me.

"Hey, are you okay?" he asked as we were about to head out on the highway. I blew on the window, and my breath fogged it in a cloud that kept me from seeing us leave. On any other day, I'd use my finger to draw a speech bubble and write something funny. Not today.

"Okay," my father said, and on any other day I would have believed him. Then he stepped on the gas pedal.

I looked out the window but saw nothing. From now on, I'd have a new address: 7 Old Sutton Road in a suburb of Chicago, IL. Hundreds of miles away from Boston and Somerville and Alex and the best of the best Massachusetts youth soccer had to offer.

I had forgotten all about it. Simple as that. Two years in the making and I had forgotten all about it. Two years ago my father and my mother had started building a house in Chicago. Their dream house in their dream suburb of their dream town with their dream job. And now we were off chasing this dream job and dream house. This morning's game against the *Brookline Soccer Sirens* had been my farewell game. And before the bus delivered the youth soccer team and before I met Alex, that was just fine by me. Chicago couldn't be worse than the *Somerville Soccer Swallows*. I could see it now. In

Chicago the girls' teams might be called *Soccer Cuties* or *Soccer Sweethearts,* and play with little pink balls, but that doesn't make icky any worse. I wanted to barf.

Talking to Alex changed everything. Now a girls' soccer team was out of the question. Sure there were good girls' teams. The Women's U.S. Soccer Team had twice won the World Cup and three times the gold medal at the Olympics, and my father never misses a chance to remind me that the U.S. Women's team did much better than the men's. But for me, playing with boys was what I wanted more than anything. I suffered through everything from Amelia Dessert to Coach Squeamish. The boys laughed at me for two years, but it didn't matter, because I knew that one day I'd make it. I knew that I was as good as the next boy, probably even better. And this morning I knew that one day my dream would come true and I'd play for the U.S. National Soccer Team. Playing with the Men's National Soccer Team was a long shot, but who knows? I might be the first girl to do that!

But every mile on the highway took me a mile further away from my dreams. As the miles wore on, I realized that I'd have to start all over again. I'd have to play on a girls' soccer team again. To be honest, I didn't want to any more. I was done. Finito! I felt like somebody had

tripped me just before the finish line. Why couldn't we stay in Boston? My mother died over a year ago. What did she care about that old dream house in Chicago now? And what did my father get out of living in a dream house in a dream town if mom was gone and I was miserable? All the money from the best dream job in the world couldn't make up for *this*. Even a big fat company car didn't help. Because if there's anything I learned in the last couple of years it's that you can't buy your dreams. You have to fight for them to make them come true. But now, sitting in this car, watching my whole world grow smaller and smaller in the distance, I just didn't have the strength and the courage to start all over again. And so, before we even left, I threw my soccer gear in the trash.

The Creepy Castle

Dusk fell and the fog rolled in. Chicago was all headlights and horns – everything else was swallowed by a thick blanket of grayish white. Finally, in Elmwood Park the blanket misted into long tattered white shreds that whooshed like dragons through the streets of the town we would now call home. No one was on the streets; nobody was walking their dog or riding their bike, just high walls of stone on both sides of the street, rising up to the treetops. It was as if we were driving through a maze of prison corridors. Where are the kids? I wondered.

My father navigated the maze, looking for a way out, I hoped, but instead, he took one of the countless corners and turned into an even smaller and quieter street. Then suddenly he stopped the car. A huge wooden gate appeared up ahead in the fog: 7 Old Sutton Road. I looked at my father for the first time since we left Boston. He bit his lip and when he felt my gaze, he turned slowly to me.

"What do you think?"

"I hate it," I said. What else could I say. My whole world was gone and he didn't even notice.

My words bit him, but he was my dad, and so he was, of course, wiser than me. "Mom knew you would say that," he said, pensive. "But she also said you would learn to love it."

I couldn't believe he said that. Tears flooded my eyes. How could he talk about Mom at a time like this? She never would have made me to move to Chicago. It was my father who was chasing his dream. Wasn't it? At that moment, I felt totally and utterly alone. He was my best friend. With Mom gone, he was the only person in the world who let me be *me*. Why was he doing this?

The wooden gate at 7 Old Sutton Road creaked open as if by magic, and the car slowly rolled into the dark cobblestone driveway. The tires clattered. The headlights invaded the darkness. Up ahead, a lantern swung in the wind and I could hear it creaking even from inside the car. It swung and creaked above a small wooden door in the house that I swear, looked more like a creepy castle than home sweet home.

The house looked crooked and twisted, even though it was brand new. The tile roof bent as if carrying the weight of five hundred years. On one side the roof touched the ground as if it walked with a crutch. Beams crisscrossed the walls like bloodlines, and windows peeked through and glared back at me. Big eyes and small eyes, some open wide, others with lids half closed, all in different shapes and sizes. This was my mother's dream house? Like I said before and I stand by it: this wasn't a dream house, it was a creepy castle.

The wind howled when I got out the car. Fall had come early this year, and the leaves whirled through the moonless night like waves of bats. Although I knew that ghosts and goblins weren't real, I rushed into the house and slammed the door shut behind me.

Bam!

My father looked at me in surprise.

The house had seemed so small outside, but inside, it was huge. And empty. Completely empty. No rugs, no furniture. Not a single picture on the wall. Nothing.

"Your mother wanted us to furnish it and decorate it together. A house needs to grow with the people who live in it. What do you say?"

What do I say? What could I say? Why should I help decorate this house? I couldn't stand being here! And so I said nothing.

"The only thing we can't touch is the kitchen. Mom said it was perfect. Everything else is up to us. Come on, Zoe. Say something." At that moment, my father smiled the smile I really don't like to see on his face. That soap bubble smile that adults flash us kids, telling us our problems seem like huge problems today, but someday will disappear, like soap bubbles, when we pop them.

"I'm tired," I said. "Where's my room?"

My father's soap bubble smile burst. He nodded sadly, grabbed my bag, and marched through the living room toward what looked from across the room like a small Alice in Wonderland door. Up close I could see that the door wasn't small at all, it just looked that way because it was at the bottom of three short stairs. My father stopped at the top and turned.

"Everything beyond this door is yours. Your rules and your laws apply."

I shrugged. I know he was trying to win me over, but to me, the door seemed more like a gate to a nasty old dungeon. My father went down the steps anyway and opened the door silently. There was no turning back.

The room behind the door was fantastic. It was wild, with five or six crooked corners, walls with lots of nooks and crannies, and ceilings that stretched to the sky. At least that's what it looked like when I first stepped into it. But then I got it: the room was in the part of the house where the roof touched the ground, and high above me the beams of the attic crossed like the crown of an ancient tree. This was the perfect place for a tree house, I thought, and a few days ago I probably would have started building one the very next day. But not now – I didn't care anymore. I walked to the mattress sprawled on the floor in the center of the room and sat down.

I'm sure my father had expected more excitement from me. But he didn't let on.

"You're having a tough time with this, aren't you?" he asked.

I just looked at my feet. I mean really. Duh.

"You know, Zoe, it's tough for me too. Both of us are starting all over again. How are we going to help each other? Let's say we're playing soccer... "

"Let's not and say we did," I said.

My father shot a glance at me the way he always did when I did something wrong. "That was rude," he said.

I knew it was rude. I was angry. He was right and I never liked it when he was right, which was a lot. "Sorry," I said.

"If you have the ball, you're on your own until someone takes it away from you. You know how it is. But your teammates can help you keep it. They can break free and block and maybe even help you get to the goal." He shrugged. "You're having a hard time, I can break free and help you. Same goes for you."

My father sat down in front of me, not getting too close. He knew I didn't want anybody in my face.

"What do you say, Zoe? Can we do this? Can we be a team?"

I slowly lifted my head and looked at him. I was hurting and really, I didn't know what to do. So I cried.

"I don't have a team anymore." My eyes burned with tears. "My team is gone."

I shoved my head into the pillows and for a moment,

everything was quiet. Then I heard my father's footsteps fade away as he left and seconds later the door slammed shut with an echoing boom. I was alone.

Horror Birthday to You!

Two hours later, I was still awake. It was almost midnight. The wind howled and whispered through the beams and I'm not going to lie, it was scary. It was like I was living in the house on haunted hill.

I'm Zoe the fearless and this is no ghost story. There went that wind again. You know, fearlessness doesn't do you any good if the situation is hopeless. Giving up is far worse than fear or dread. Giving up is weak; it makes you feel small and helpless. And if you feel small and helpless, fear catches up with you. Fear like you've never felt before, mean and monstrous.

The wind whispered and howled; it was creepy. At thirty seconds to midnight, thirty seconds to my ninth birthday, I closed my eyes and wished a horrible monster would come get me and put me out of my misery. Or maybe come and save me. If I sounded crazy, that's because I was. I was in a new town in a new house in a new room where the wind was playing tricks with my mind. New rule: be careful what you wish for.

The wind howled and whispered, the shutters rattled, the beams creaked and moaned. When the hands of the clock moved to midnight, church bells chimed from far away; too far to protect me. I could hear shuffling steps coming closer and closer and then they stopped just outside my door.

Red smoke seeped through the keyhole and the cracks underneath my door. Somebody pushed down the handle with a creak. I held my breath and played dead. A nanosecond later the door flew open, and a blinding light pierced the fiery smoke that billowed into my room. A bone-chilling roar chased the smoke and light all the way to my mattress. I could see it standing in the door frame: two horns atop a huge head, green eyes, and sharp claws on hairy paws. A monster.

"Stay calm! This is not real!" I told myself as the monster roared louder. It roared and roared, and then it stomped into my room.

Galumph! Galumph! The monster feet stomped on the old wooden slats. *Galumph! Galumph! Galumph!* The monster thundered directly towards me. *Galumph! Galumph! Galumph! Galumph!* Ten more steps tops until it would reach me, and as if to mock me, it snapped its claws in rhythm with its steps. *Galumph! Snap! Galumph! Galumph! Snap!* I could see its powerful fangs clearly now, and I'm telling you, these fangs didn't lose any of their horror when the monster suddenly began to sing.

"Heyheyhey!" The monster kept the eerie rhythm.
"Heyheyhey!" *Galumph! Snap! Galumph!*

"Heyheyhey and Happy Birthday!" *Galumph! Snap! Galumph! Galumph! Snap!* "Happy Birthday! Happy Birthday! Happyyyy! ROAR!"

The monster tore open its mouth. It was directly above me, its powerful fangs ready to rip into me. That's when I saw my father's face, hidden behind the darkness of the mask, grinning through those gigantic horrifying yellow fangs. At the same time the monster shoved something into my face. It looked like a brightly burning black soccer ball. It was a chocolate birthday cake with nine candles on top, all of them lit.

"Happy birthday, my darling!" my father laughed and the monster head laughed too.

But I didn't take the cake right away. No way!

"Dad, I thought you were going to give me a heart attack!" I pouted. "Are you trying to make fun of me?"

I spun and hid beneath my blanket. My father took off the monster head and sat down next to me on the bed.

"I don't get it, tiger," he said. "The most exciting year of your life is about to begin and you're trying to miss it."

I rolled my eyes.

"A cake and a monster mask? How is that exciting? Scary, maybe, but exciting? I don't think so! You're hopeless!"

"No, you are," my father said, squinting at me. At least I think he was squinting. I don't know for sure because I was still spun around from him, but that's usually what he did when I told him he was hopeless and he said, "No, you are."

"I'm not talking about cakes or monsters," he said. "I'm talking about your new soccer team."

That got my attention. I turned around slowly. Now it was my turn to squint. In fact, I went all snake-eyes on him. "What are you talking about?" I said.

"Nothing much to tell, tiger. Your first practice is today."

I sighed and spun away from him once more. Here we go, I thought. Another pink fru-fru team, this time from the sugar and spice windy city, all pink high-tops and jerseys with rhinestones and screaming, giggling girls keeping me from my dream.

"And what's the name of the team *this* time? *The Soccer Sweethearts?*" Sheesh. What I don't need is another girls' team in a new town. What was I going to do? Nothing could replace that boys' team back in Somerville.

My father laughed. "*Soccer Sweethearts.* But do us *both* a favor and don't mention that name around the boys. I don't think they'll appreciate it, especially since it's not a sure thing you're even going to make the team."

"Wait a minute, Dad!" I yelled and spun back around. "Did you just say – *boys?*"

My father grinned. "Good. Your hearing still works. But I'm warning you – this is a real team. They're called *The Wild Soccer Bunch,* but I hear the name isn't half as tough as they are."

"Really tough, huh?" I asked. "How do *you* know?"

"Their coach and I go way back."

"Tomorrow, huh?" I was getting really excited now.

"It's not tomorrow anymore. It's today at four o'clock," my father said, and checked his watch. "You have exactly 15 hours and 58 minutes to get ready."

I was suddenly on my feet and I swear I don't know how I got there. "Holy Goalie! A real boys' team! Dad! Why didn't you *say* so?!"

"I think I just did," my father said.

"I mean, why didn't you say it *before* I threw everything I owned in the trash?"

"You're kidding, right?" It was a fair question. I just didn't want to answer it.

"Well, I, kinda threw all my soccer gear into the trash," I said, finally.

"When did you have time to do that? We just got here!"

"Not here, Dad. Back in Boston."

My father gasped. "You didn't."

I nodded real fast, like a bobble-headed doll.

"Zoe." He couldn't believe his ears. "Everything you owned was soccer gear. All your school clothes, everything," he said. Then he muttered to himself, "I guess that explains why you didn't have a suitcase."

I nodded even faster and I must have looked crazed because he immediately backed away from me and got out of range. He knew I sometimes pounded my fists on things whenever I got excited, and boy was I excited. But, seeing as this was a new house in a new town, I decided to try something different. I took a deep breath instead and said calmly: "And that would also explain why the neighbor's trashcans were so full. We probably ought to call them and apologize. And while we're at it, see if my stuff is still in there? Maybe they can dig it out?"

"I guess it's a good thing I noticed the bulging trash

cans and dug them out," my father said, grinning. He raced across the room and grabbed something just outside the door, then came back and dropped a familiar duffel bag in front of me.

I was speechless.

My father burst out laughing. "This belong to you, young lady?"

"No young ladies here, Dad," I replied, pretending to get all serious.

"You're hopeless!"

"No, you are," I said and flashed my best smile. He scooched over to me and put his arm around me and it felt like he was going to crush me. "Well, I can't argue with that. Looks like we're both hopeless. I guess we deserve each other!"

I leaned my head against him. It had been a long time since I did that.

My smile became even more triumphant and my father scratched his ear. "Of course, all that stuff is dirty and needs to be washed, which means you still don't have anything to wear tomorrow. Am I right or am I right?"

My smile vanished. "Hmm," he grumbled. "I guess that means no practice today – unless you stop moping and start celebrating your birthday."

With that, he pulled a present out of the monster

head and held it out to me. "What do you say? Want to try having a good time?"

I considered it. That is, I acted as if I was considering it. Truth is, I was so excited I could barely stand still. "Okay!" I yelled and tore the present from my father's hands. It was soft and flat. I ripped the wrapping paper as if I was the monster. Then I held it up to see. It was a brand-new U.S. Mens' National Team jersey with the number five and my name on the back.

"Awesome!" I exclaimed and put it on. "How did you get it? You can't just walk in and buy these, you know!"

"True. I made it part of my deal. Like the company car."

"No way."

"Okay, you got me, maybe it wasn't part of the deal, but you have it and that means I got it for you. So, just figure your dad has connections, how's that?" My father flashed me a big smile. "You're going to have to get your own cleats, though, and that's not going to be easy. Grandma Kate is coming tomorrow morning and you know how she feels about girls playing soccer."

"Grandma? Here?" I gasped. "Really?"

"Afraid so," my father sighed. "And no funny stuff; your mom wouldn't appreciate you playing tricks on her own mother."

I shrugged. "I would never do anything like that," I said.

My dad rolled his eyes. "Let me remind about the shaving cream in the hand while she was sleeping? Does that sound familiar?"

"That was so long ago. What was I? Eight?"

"Yeah. It was last month. Just knock it off."

"No problem," I said, admiring the jersey again. "Why is she coming anyway? We don't need her here, do we?"

"She thinks we do. New house, new town. You know the drill."

"Great," I sighed. "With Grandma, resistance is futile."

My father shrugged. "Exactly."

"As long as she doesn't make me wear a dress, we'll be fine."

My father made a funny face like he'd just sucked a lemon and I laughed. "Yeah, that would be devastating, wouldn't it? Don't worry. I have your back. I'll tell you what. I'm going to go out on a limb for you. I'm going to tell her *exactly* what you need."

"Really, you'd do that?" I asked. I was really surprised.

"What do you think? I'm your father. It's my job!"

"She's not going to like it when you get to the word 'cleats'," I said.

"How can she say no?" he said. "It's not every day her

only granddaughter turns nine!"

I hugged my father and kissed his cheek like some wild child and didn't let go. "I love you, Daddy! And you know what else? If Grandma Kate takes over you, I'll do everything I can to bring you back!"

"Well, I appreciate that, tiger," my father said. "But before we do battle with Grandma, how about a last meal? I vote for a piece of cake!"

He sure deserved some cake, but first I had to make a wish. I closed my eyes and imagined my mother was with us. I imagined taking her hand and then taking my father's hand. Then I made my wish: to be forever as happy as I was at that moment.

I blew out the candles, all nine of them at the same time. Then we dug our hands into the cake. Yes, we ate it with our bare hands, licking our fingers, and laughing at what Grandma would say if she saw us. Then I brushed my teeth, kissed my father one more time, rolled over in my jersey, and listened to the groaning and creaking and moaning of the house. It wasn't creepy any more. It was playing a wild birthday song, lulling me to sleep and into a cool dream about living in a tree house between the attic beams in my new room.

Grandma Comes to Creepy Castle

I slept late the next morning. I was exhausted from
the day before, but I felt great after my midnight
birthday party with my father. It was about eleven when
I stumbled into the kitchen, sleepy and a little lost,
looking for the refrigerator.

"Oh dear, dear, dear, look what the cat dragged in!"

I recognized the voice immediately. I turned slowly.
The woman who belonged to the voice wore a pink
leisure suit with matching hat and carried a fake
leather bag.

"Oh, hi Grandma! How sweet of you to drop by and
wish me a happy birthday." My sweet-talking voice was
covered in chocolate syrup.

Grandma scrunched up her face and grimaced.
"Well, it was kind of hard to do, seeing as you've been
sleeping most of the day away!" she snapped at me
and gave me the once over, no doubt noticing my every
fashion offense: tangled hair, soccer jersey, and my
dad's untied boots, which I wore because I couldn't

find my slippers. "I came to see my granddaughter, not some gross goblin!" Grandma turned up her nose. My father, who was sitting at the breakfast table, tried to avoid eye contact, but got hit by her glance of disdain and contempt. "Or do you somehow believe this critter that stands before us looks like a girl?" She didn't let my father answer. Instead, she carried on: "No, Scott-Francis, this creature is practically a boy and I'm warning you here and now, you will completely ruin her without a woman in the house."

My father almost choked on his breakfast. Grandma was never one to mince words. Maybe that's where I got it. Who knows? My father was too polite to argue and gently waved her off. "And who do you recommend, Kate?" My father teased.

"Why, me, of course," my grandma played along. "Rebecca would want nothing less." Then she got real sad thinking about my mother and looked away so we wouldn't see. "It's been more than a year. And well, Rebecca's gone, and now it's up to us to make sure our little Zoe gets a decent upbringing. And you, Zoe, you can't just straddle the fence all your life. Boys are boys and girls are girls and never the twain shall meet. Ahem. Until later in life, of course." When she turned back to us, I could see she had been crying and she wiped a pesky tear from her face. "After all, I didn't try to become a heavyweight champion, either."

"Phew! Lucky for Muhammad Ali!" I grinned, broke the fifth egg into the mixer and turned on the machine. Grandma was horrified.

"Oh dear, dear, dear! What on earth are you doing?"

"Fixing breakfast," I answered dryly.

"But it's already on the table, Zoe!" Grandma complained.

Yep. There it was. A pink birthday cake, courtesy of Grandma Kate. I had to think fast. I didn't want to say what I really meant.

"Hey! It matches your outfit!" Then I turned off the mixer, took off the lid, put it to my lips, emptied it in one long gulp, and a burp came out of me before I could stop it. "Excuse me," I said.

Grandma shot me a look. "I thought you'd dig pink," she said. "Right?"

"Sorry, Grandma," I said. "But pink Barbie doll frosting is really not my thing." I said this calmly and sweetly with the voice of an angel. It took Grandma at least 15 seconds – a new record – to answer.

"Suit yourself," she threw her head back, clearly insulted. "I suppose you won't like your birthday present either."

"As long as it's not pink," I blurted out. Oops. What can I say? I was relieved. I slowly approached the present on the table, like it was my prey. I knew what I asked for and I knew dad said he was going to go out on a limb, but in my family things take weird turns all the time, so if I was getting dress shoes, I prayed they were not pink. I ripped open the present and inside was a shoebox; so far so good. Slowly, I opened the lid and looked inside and there they were: a beautiful pair of red soccer cleats.

I was stunned. They were perfect.

"Red, of all things!" Grandma shook her head. "And I'll go to the North Pole before I return them, so you better fall in love with them right here and now! It was embarrassing enough buying them. Everyone looked at me funny!"

I'm sure they didn't. Grandma had a wild imagination like me. I looked at my father: "And she didn't kill you when you asked her?"

My father grinned and shook his head. "Nope. Not even a little torture. She might have put a curse on me, but I didn't feel it."

I gave my father a smile of thanks, then said to Grandma: "Thank you!" I snatched the soccer cleats out of the shoe box and threw my arms around my grandmother's neck. "You know what, Grandma? Sometimes you are the best grandma in the whole wide world.

"You actually *like* them?" she asked me.

"They are awesomazing!" She looked at me, confused, so I continued: "Exactly what I wanted!" She looked relieved.

I hugged my grandmother as hard as I could and planted kisses all over her face. She looked at my father, perplexed.

"So?" my father grinned back at her. "What's it like being kissed by a goblin?"

My grandma turned up her nose with a harumph and I

laughed. "Depends on which one you think is the goblin."

"I'm warning you!" My grandma complained, but then she hugged me so tight that I could barely breathe.

Close Encounters
of a Different Kind

The rain and fog of the night before had disappeared;
Chicago gave me a beautiful and sunny fall day for my
birthday. I felt fantastic and I couldn't wait to go to
the practice with the *Wild Soccer Bunch*. When it was
finally a quarter to four, I got into my father's car. I was
wearing my brand new U.S. Soccer jersey and the red
soccer cleats, and I was ready to jump out of my skin.

Grandma sadly waved goodbye as if I was headed
for some kind of death march, but I didn't care. I knew
better. I was headed for my first practice with a boys'
team. Let me tell you, I'd been waiting for this moment
for years. It was finally going to happen and I couldn't
wait to get out there on the field and show them what
I had. Yes, I couldn't wait all right. Except when we
got there, I froze and couldn't get out of the car. I just
stared at the gate of the wooden fence that kept the
Wild Soccer Bunch from view.

"Hey, are you okay?" my father asked at a quarter past

four as I chewed my fingernails. I fidgeted and chewed for another five minutes and finally my father had had enough and he brought out the big guns: "How about I go with you? You know, just for moral support. I mean who wouldn't be nervous and afraid..."

"I'm not afraid!" I said, angrily cutting him off, not moving one iota. "I'm not..."

"Sure, Zoe, anything you say," my father answered dutifully, leaning past me and opening the passenger door. "But I'm coming with you if I don't see you disappear behind that wooden gate in twenty seconds."

"Yes, Sir!" I nodded and looked at the second hand of the clock on the dashboard. After fifteen seconds, my right foot touched ground outside the car. "You sure they know I'm coming today?"

"Yes, I called the coach myself," my father assured me. "His name is Larry."

"Larry what?" I was biding time.

"Not Squeamish or Monstrous, just Larry," my father smiled. I loved this smile. It was his 'I-got-your-back-no-matter-what' smile. "Now get going. I'll pick you up later in the afternoon." And so, armed with my father's smile and a thumping heart, I pecked him on the cheek and finally got out of the car. He pulled the door shut as I stood there, just in case I changed my mind, I guess. So I spun on my heel and walked through the wooden gate to face my destiny.

As soon as I passed through the gate, for a very brief moment, I caught a glimpse of the *Wild Soccer Bunch* practicing on the field.

Eleven boys, all in black with bright orange socks. This brief moment was enough for me to see what a good team they were. And when I said a brief moment, I meant a brief moment because in the *next* moment, the entire field went silent. I swear even the birds stopped chirping. Everyone and everything went totally still, as if time had stopped. Even the ball seemed to hover in the air above our heads.

I felt like I was in the zoo. Everyone stared at me like I was some weird cross between a kangaroo and a crocodile. It felt familiar, because that's how everyone has always stared at me my whole life. And so I was the first to get over it. I cleared my throat and bravely asked for Larry. Everyone else was still frozen in time. Seemed like they'd stay that way forever.

"Hello, my name is Zoe," I repeated. "My father called Larry and he said I could play with you?"

I waited. Then time jolted forward for a quarter of a second, and in that quarter of a second all eleven wild guys threw their heads to the left. I followed their glances and saw Larry for the first time. He was sitting on the grass, cross-legged, grinning at me.

"Hello, Zoe," he greeted me. "You're late!"

Time resumed and the laws of gravity kicked in and the ball plummeted to the earth with a whistle and hit one of the *Wild Soccer Bunch,* the one with the number 13, right on the head. Boing!

"Hold it right there, Larry! You really know this girl?" Number 13 had returned to the living.

"Sure," Larry said. "This is Zoe. Zoe Burns. Didn't I just tell you?" He got up and approached me.

"Yeah, you said some words," the boy snorted. "But, well, did you happen to notice she's a --- girl?!"

"Very good, Kevin!" Larry mocked him. "Did you figure that out all by yourself?"

Kevin, flustered, gestured with his hand, then spun to the guy next to him and said, "Danny, say something! Larry is about to put a girl on our team."

But Danny, the boy with number 4 on his back, didn't say a word. For him, time also still stood still. I could almost hear the music. He stared at me as if I was Santa Claus and the Easter Bunny all rolled into one. To be honest, he didn't look too bright at that moment.

"Dude!" Kevin shouted. "This is bad luck, man. Like women on those old boats. It's like a curse!"

"Really?" Danny asked with a smile that made him look like he just got struck by a bolt of lightning.

"Yeah! I'm pretty sure!" Kevin said. "Guys! Have you

all lost your minds?"

"Mind?" Danny grinned. "I don't have a mind."

A boy with red hair and coke bottle glasses jumped forward. "Kevin is right. This is all wrong!"

"You got that right!" the smallest one chimed in. "Wrong as in there is nothing right about it. Not since *I* joined the *Wild Soccer Bunch!* And that's been like almost my whole life!"

"Exactly!" The others chimed in, too, and finally one of them added, "Larry, I'm warning you! You let her join the team, I'm out."

Crystal clear and razor sharp, it hit me right in the heart. And this was from the oldest and the tallest of the bunch. And he was totally *serious*.

"My brother Tyler is right!" Kevin shouted. "If she plays with us, we are gone."

It suddenly got quiet again. All I could hear was my heartbeat and Larry's cap as he pushed it back to squint at me. Then he sighed, turned to the others and said, "Okay, okay! I get it, and I'm real sorry, too. I should have asked you first. I know doggone it, but I didn't. I didn't think you'd get so riled up over a girl. I thought you guys were beyond that. And well, now you see, I'm in kind of a bind here. Zoe's dad and I go way back and I promised him that she could train with us. See if she liked it."

"See if *she* liked it?" Kevin asked. "What about us?"

"What about you?" Larry asked. "What if she's *good?*"

"How could she be?" asked Tyler.

It was right about here that I was thinking maybe the boys of Chicago were less evolved than the boys of Boston, but I kept my mouth shut. I was nine now and needed to act more grown up.

"You gonna help me keep my word or not?" Larry asked.

The *Wild Soccer Bunch* looked at him in disbelief.

"But there's rules against it," Kevin said and all the other guys nodded in agreement. Everyone except Danny. "Aren't there?"

"Actually," Larry said, "there ain't." He shoved his hands in his pockets. "Come on, give her a chance," he pleaded. "If she can't play, we send her home."

"And what if she *can* play?" Kevin asked. "*Then* what happens?"

Larry shrugged. "Then we lose a perfectly good player, all because she's a girl."

He shot me a glance, and then turned back to Kevin. "What do you say, Kev? All of you? Do we get past this? Or do we wait until next year when you're a little more... grown up?"

Kevin said nothing, but all the guys felt the challenge in Larry's voice. I sure did, so they *must* have. Kevin looked me up and down. It made me nervous and I bit my lip, hoping it wasn't already bloody. Kevin knew I was feeling kind of small then, I could tell by the way he looked me over and that's when I knew I was in trouble.

"Deal," Kevin said, smiling at me like he had just signed my death sentence. "One practice, one tryout," Kevin continued. "To make the team, you gotta pass the test."

Then he assigned teams.

Boys Are Total Losers!

Of course, I was on Kevin and Tyler's team, the two guys who screamed the loudest to keep me out. Why does it always work out that way? The other members of my team were no better, believe me. There was Roger, the redhead with the coke bottle glasses. He looked like he had been through something traumatic with a stylist. Who cut his hair? Pre-schoolers? He couldn't stand me, pure and simple. Josh, the smallest of the bunch, was a mean garden gnome, and Fabio, oh so gorgeous Fabio, was all business. Of course, he didn't bother counting me in. "We are playing five on six," he turned to Larry. "We get the ball."

Larry gave him a look, then just nodded. He didn't say anything and I knew I'd have to get used to that. Coach Squeamish would have benched Fabio for bad sportsmanship. But I was no longer with the sweet *Somerville Swallows*. I was in the real rough and tough world of the wild, the world I had longed for my whole life. And this world wasn't known for its manners and courtesy. Larry scratched his head and handed the ball to Fabio.

"Okay! Let's start," Kevin shouted. "No more than three ball contacts per player. You get that?" he asked me.

"I only get to touch the ball three times, including stopping and passing, right?"

Kevin seemed surprised for a moment. But then he caught himself and got that mean look again. "Wow. You know your terms. Let's see if you can play." Point for Kevin. This was going to be tough.

"Okay, Phooey, or whatever your name is. You'll play left forward with Fabio and me."

"It's Zoe," I said. Of course, it had to be left, I thought. Why not just tie my feet together? But I was Zoe the fearless after all, and so I dutifully marched toward my position, seething inside. You wait, I thought. I'll show you!

I never even got the chance. Larry's whistle blew and Kevin, Tyler, Roger, Josh, and Fabio played five on six. In other words, they played like I wasn't even there. Even when I was absolutely free right in front of the goal and yelled like a crazy person, they just played around me. And worse, they scored every time, without my help. They made it very clear they didn't need me.

But I was still Zoe the fearless, and so I didn't give up.

"Bravo!" I applauded when it was five-zero for our team. "You guys are really chillax! I mean, I can barely tell you are scared of me! You're doing a fantastic job of faking it."

The *Wild Soccer Bunch* just looked at me, then laughed. "You hear that, men?" Kevin and Tyler shouted, but I cut off their laughter. "I think they heard me loud and clear, but if they didn't I'll be glad to repeat it. Men. Or whatever it is you think you are."

"I'll tell you what we're *not*. We're not afraid," Roger said.

"I think you are. I think you're afraid I might be good." Kevin laughed again. "You're crazy."

"Oh yeah?" I snapped. "Then why didn't you ever pass to me?"

That shut them up.

I looked over at Larry. He was amused to say the least and shot me a thumbs-up. That gave me courage. I couldn't hide my delight. I had hit them where it hurt the most, and Kevin and the *Wild Soccer Bunch* were not only shaking in their cleats, they were boiling with anger.

"Whatever." Kevin accepted the challenge. "Let's see who laughs last."

Then as soon as we started the game up again, Kevin passed the ball to me so hard there was no way I could stop it. The ball bounced, and drifted all the way to the other side and the other team scored. Just my luck! My mistake led to their first goal. Kevin grinned so I turned my back on him, but I could still feel his gaze burning into my back. The same thing happened two more times. Even though it was never my fault, and even though Kevin, Tyler, and Fabio did their best to get me to mess up, I could feel my confidence getting knocked down with every shot. So when Tyler finally sent a perfect pass my way, I totally messed up.

It was five-four when I finally got the ball in front of our own penalty box, but I was in such a tight spot, there was no way I could pass it. Joey, who plays as if he put a spell on the ball, Diego the tornado, and Julian Fort Knox, the all-in-one defender, surrounded me. I

58

tried to break free, but the others just counted my ball touches – out loud. It was insulting. The best dribbling in all nine years of my life, but nobody cared. What was the matter with these guys? When I touched the ball the fourth time, Larry whistled and the other team got a free kick. At that moment, Alex jogged up front. Josh explained that Alex "the cannon" was the man with the hardest kick in the world. He left no room for doubt. He pounded the ball into the net so hard it toppled over. Five-five. Tie score.

"Bravo! Bravo!" Kevin shouted and applauded. "Great playing, Phooey!"

"Zoe," I said dryly. "Right. Five-zero to five-five – in less than five minutes. A new record, right, Larry?"

Larry just rolled his eyes. The others roared with laughter. Kevin stepped up to me and whispered so only I could hear, "Get lost."

Let me tell you something. I was totally ready to get lost at that moment, but Kevin must have seen the pain in my face because he backed down and decided he wasn't done with me. "What the heck, men," he yelled mockingly. "It's not her fault. She's a girl."

That's when Danny stepped in, "Let's give her another chance. We can decide the match in penalty kicks just like we always do."

I looked over at Larry the coach who was nodding to himself. I guess he approved.

Kevin glared at Danny, but what could he do. That's how it's done and he couldn't back down. "Sure," he said. "And Phooey-"

"Zoe," I corrected him.

"Whatever. You'll do all five kicks for us. That okay with you, Larry?"

Larry crossed his arms. "It's up to you, Zoe."

I think at that moment Larry knew the team was so mad at him for saddling them with a girl that he wouldn't lift a finger to help me. Since I knew there weren't going to be any magic fairies showing up to magically fix this one for me, I was on my own. But Larry was right. I needed to take matters in my own hands. I had to prove myself, to me and to the others. And I would. Yes, I would. I could feel my heart pounding in my chest. I was scared, all right. I kept hearing his voice in my head: "Get lost. Get lost..."

But it was too late. Joey made his first penalty shot and scored. Then Kevin was about to put the ball down for me, but I couldn't let him do that, so I rushed over, grabbed the ball from his hands, and put it down myself. I could hear the others murmur, and my legs wobbled. I tried to concentrate. I moved into position in a curved line so that it would look like I was going to use my right foot to pound the ball into the left corner. But I planned to switch legs at the last moment and take a shot with the outside of my left foot into the right corner. That was the plan. But the moment I got ready for the shot, the ground seemed to shake and I hesitated for a nanosecond too long and the next thing I knew I didn't catch the ball at the right angle and it hammered against the post.

My second penalty shot missed the goal by a mile. As usual, Diego scored, and it was two-zero against us. Against me, was more like it, because I don't think there was anyone on my side.

Or so I thought.

Danny prepared his ball and for some weird reason his face was red. He wouldn't look at me. He was so distracted when he charged and kicked the ball that, like me, he thundered it way over the goal.

"What was *that!?*" Kevin was shocked, but Danny just shrugged as he passed his teammate and Kevin grabbed him. "What do you think you're doing? Do you actually *like* her? Are you crushing on her?" Danny responded instantly with a shot to Kevin's stomach that doubled him over.

"Don't ever say that again," Danny spat. "I missed on purpose. Gotta keep the suspense going, right?"

Kevin's pained face managed a smile when he realized what Danny was saying. "Keep the suspense going. Good idea. Did you hear that, Kyle?" he called out to the goalie. "Let one in! Or else the girl doesn't stand a chance."

"No problem," Kyle responded. "But she's gotta be able to hit the ball."

The *Wild Soccer Bunch* roared with laughter and my nerves tightened like a rubber band. "Get lost get lost get lost!" The echo in my head of Kevin's meanness got louder and louder and I had to fight back the tears. No way was I going to cry. I wasn't going to do them any favors.

I took a deep breath and charged and the ball went straight at the goalie. Kyle could have caught it easily, but instead, jumped out of the way in horror, like it was a cannonball coming straight at him. Did I mention Kyle was a lousy actor?

"Hey! What did I say? Two-one! Did you see that? I bet that was the penalty kick of the century." The *Wild Soccer Bunch* pretended to cheer for me, and I cursed them silently for doing this to me. It was humiliating and I secretly wiped a tear from my face.

Then Julian Fort Knox missed the next penalty kick and it was obvious what he was doing, especially when he had to hold his stomach he was laughing so hard. I, on the other hand, delivered *such* a good shot that this time Kyle "the invincible" – yes, this is really what he called himself – Kyle didn't have to help me score. Kevin wasn't impressed. He ran to Alex, the man with the hardest kick in the world, and whispered in his ear. Alex smiled his famously silent grin and mixed it with a dash of hostility. Then he charged, took a shot and, as if it was pulled by a magnet, the ball hurled against the post.

The *Wild Soccer Bunch* cheered and fell on the ground, laughing. Alex was too good a shot for that to have been an accident. He did it on purpose and that destroyed my last bit of confidence. How could I think I could play with a bunch of boys who could hit the crossbar on purpose? I wanted to run, but before I had a chance to take off, Kevin shoved a soccer ball in my face.

"So, who's afraid now?" His eyes fixed on me while mine welled up with tears.

"It's all up to you!" Kevin continued, obviously enjoying his power. "Maybe you need a tissue to wipe your eyes first?"

Fail! That hurt. I closed my eyes. Pull yourself together! I pleaded with myself, gearing up for one last pep talk. I am Zoe the fearless. It is what mom always called me. What are you waiting for? Let's do this. I opened my eyes, grabbed the ball from Kevin's hands, and placed it on the penalty spot. But as I walked backwards, the ground underneath me seemed to soften.

As I charged, the ground felt like it was trying to trip me. And then the fake cheering from the *Wild Soccer Bunch* finished the job. When I was about to kick the ball with my right foot, everything, absolutely everything – the ground, the cheers, my entire life – crashed in on me. I couldn't focus. I lost my balance, missed the ball, and fell flat on my back.

Time stood still.

I was spread-eagled on my back in the dirt and I didn't want to move. I wanted to sink into the center of the earth and disappear forever. I could feel the tears coming again and I didn't think I could stop them. Maybe they'd call me a crybaby; I didn't care anymore. That's what kept running through my head when suddenly Kevin appeared, towering over me. His glare was cold and full of contempt. Then he spat into the grass. You know, the way boys spit when they are pretending to be men?

"So, what do you think, Phooey?"

"Zoe," I said softly.

"Whatever," he said. "What do you think? Did you pass the test?"

I tried to hold it together, I swear. I tried to look him right in the eye and give it right back to him. If I was a boy who thought he was a man, I would have spit in his eye. But I couldn't. And I couldn't hold back the flood either. And so I did the only thing I could do: I jumped to my feet and ran away.

Don't Let the Bubble Burst

I ran through the gate and across the parking lot.
My father's car was not there because it was still too
early to pick me up so I ran and ran and ran without
looking back. And after a jillion wrong turns in this
mean old town, I finally found the house that was
masquerading as my new house. It was definitely not
a home. It was back to being a creepy castle. I hated
it. There wasn't much I didn't hate at that moment and
my father was lucky I didn't run into him first. Instead,
I ran into Grandma, who had mercifully forgotten our
morning disagreement and had devoted herself to more
important things in life.

Clad in her knightly but quite unshining armor – a
rubber apron to protect her precious pink leisure suit,
a scarf on her head doubling as a helmet, and the long
garden shears she brandished in her hand like a sword –
she had declared war on the weeds in our backyard. She
stood there on the terrace, determination in her eyes,
and a stature weird enough to scare every dandelion

into submission. She didn't even have to bend down. She just looked at them and snapped her shears and they cowered in terror.

But then she saw my face and everything changed. "Oh heaven's, dear, dear, dear, you look like you have just gone through the wringer!" Did I mention Grandma was a mind reader? "Come here and let me hug you!" She spread her angel wings and wrapped me in them. But Grandma was no angel. She looked more like an old pink duck in a rubber apron. Was it mean to call her old? I'm sorry, but it wasn't long before I realized she had no idea what was going on with me. "You can't straddle the fence, I told you so," she quacked on. "Perhaps you see what I mean now. Tomorrow we'll give this awful jersey and these awful cleats to charity."

That was just too much. I couldn't breathe. Suddenly all I could see was pink. All around me. I felt like I was being turned into a pink Barbie doll. I couldn't handle it. I was Zoe the fearless. I was going to be a great soccer star, so I tore away and ran straight to my room, slammed the door, and plopped down on my bed like an Indian guru and stayed that way until my father came home from work.

It was almost dark when he came into my room and sat down next to me.

"Hey. You weren't at the field when I came by to pick you up."

"I don't want to talk about it," I said. "And no, I didn't cry all the way home."

My father smiled. "Okay. Hey. I talked to Larry. He thinks you put up a good fight."

"Not good *enough*," I pouted.

"I'm supposed to tell you that the dribble he had to whistle off was fantastic. Better than Kevin's, and he's the best."

"Kevin! That loser?" I couldn't even stand hearing his name again. A tear had stolen its way into my eyes and I wiped it off, annoyed. "I'll never go back there again."

My father just looked at me.

"I want to go home!" My voice quivered.

"This is your home now," my father said.

"No. This is mom's home, not mine," I said, wiping my tears again. What was up with them, they just wouldn't stop.

"It was her dream," my father said.

I couldn't stop the flood. I sunk into my father's arms and started bawling. "I have dreams too, Daddy."

"And what's your dream? To give up?"

My heart stopped. Whose side was he *on?* I just wanted to go back to Somerville so I could play soccer. At least the people back there treated me like a human being. How's that giving up? "They were so mean to me, Daddy, you couldn't believe it."

"Well, I'm sorry to hear that, tiger, but let's think about this a sec," my father said. "If we were to go to Somerville right this minute, would you be able to forget about what happened today?"

I thought about it while I glared at him. Of course not. I'll never forget. And that's exactly why I wanted to go back to Somerville. I was trying to figure out what my father wanted to do. Then it hit me. He wanted to stay in Chicago, and he didn't care about what I thought one bit. Well, I wasn't going to let him walk all over me that easily. "Just to make this crystal clear, *Father*," I said icily and sat up straight to show my determination. "If we can't go home, then I'm never going to play soccer again!"

My father lowered his gaze. "That's not a dream. It's

a nightmare." He seemed really unhappy all of a sudden.
"This is really sad, you know," he said and locked eyes
with me. "You're making me decide your dreams for you.
Dreams are precious. You should never give them up.
I mean, if you give up your dreams, you lose yourself.
Here one minute. Poof! Gone the next. Like a soap
bubble. Your mother knew that. That's why she built this
home even though she knew she was dying. She knew
she'd never live here, but it made her happy knowing we
would. She did it for you, Zoe."

At that moment, I had never been more confused in
all the 3,285 days I had been alive. "If that's what mom
thought and what she did, then what should *I* do?"

"What should you do?" my father responded. "Show
the *Wild Soccer Bunch* what's what. Make them give you
a birthday present. Challenge them to a tournament."

"Me?! Them?! They won't even show up!"

"They will. Guaranteed." My father smiled. "But you're
going to have to choose your words wisely."

My father knew just what to say. It wasn't fair. But he
was my dad after all. And that was his job. I wiped the
tears from my face. "Okay. Fine," I agreed. "But once I
do this, promise me something."

"Anything."

"Promise we'll talk about Somerville," I said. "Deal?"

"It's a deal, tiger," my father said. "That is, if you still remember where it is."

I flashed him one of my best smiles.

Low Down and Dirty

The next day I marched through the neighborhood, eleven invitations in my pocket. I was in a great mood. I didn't go to the soccer field, where I could have delivered all eleven letters at once, but I went to the home of each and every member of the *Wild Soccer Bunch*. I wanted to savor the moment. I had carefully planned the order of my visits.

Roger was first. Roger, the hero. But Roger didn't look much like a hero when he opened the door of 1236 Oak Park Avenue. In fact, horror was written all over his face; horror, because I was actually standing on his doorstep and horror because he thought all girls were poison. I responded to his horror with a sugarcoated smile as I offered him the invitation to my birthday party.

"What do you say, Roger?" I asked with that same smile. "Do you have the guts to show up?" I shoved the letter at him.

Roger just stared at it. Then he stared at me, and

slammed the door in my face. I shrugged and put the letter into his mailbox. Then I marched off.

Everything went according to plan. Paying him a visit first had been the right choice. I was sure that within the next 30 seconds he'd alert the rest of the team about what I was doing. I knew they'd be waiting for me. I felt like the guy in the game Minecraft, charging through the neighborhoods, rebuilding my dreams, and closing in on my next victim.

At 1 Woodlawn Avenue, Alex tore open the door before my finger could press the doorbell, snatched the letter from my hand, and slammed the door in my face. I caught a glimpse of him in those few seconds. He looked like a shooting star, ready to fizzle out.

Next was Kyle's mansion. Actually, it's his parents' mansion, but who's arguing. I was about to ring the bell when Kyle and his father drove up – in a fancy black limo. Kyle got out, all cool and talking on his cell. I was sure the call was about me. He didn't even look up at me. He acted as if I wasn't even there, and talked right through me. "Oh, Edgar," he addressed his butler, "I'm tied up right now, would you mind taking the mail for me?"

That said, he disappeared into the house. But a second later his head popped back out and he added: "Oh, and have her leave the letter for Joey as well.

He's on his way over to get it." I learned later that Joey and his mom lived in a nearby trailer park in a van. That's actually kind of cool because they can go wherever they want *whenever* they want.

Edgar, the butler, waited in case Kyle had another instruction for him. Then he turned to me with a smile. "Oh dear, Mademoiselle. Vat did you doo wiz ze *Vild Soccer Bunch?*"

"Nothing," I responded with a smile. "Yet." Then I handed him the two letters and left, my head held high.

At 11 St. Charles Street it was Diego's mother, Mrs. Hernandez, who opened the door. I introduced myself and politely asked if Diego was there, but suddenly he wasn't at home anymore. Instead, a man's voice, way too deep, answered from inside the apartment.

"Just a moment, Mom, I mean, Mrs. Hernandez, let me see if your son is in."

Diego's mother rolled her eyes. "Well, thank you very much for letting me know you're not home," she answered the deep voice. "Please tell yourself to not be such a chicken and get out here, pronto!"

We stood there, Diego's mother and I, for what seemed like an eternity, waiting for a reply. It finally came, "I'm so sorry, Mrs. Hernandez, but I just can't seem to find myself right now."

I burst out laughing. That was just too funny. Mrs. Hernandez was amused as well. "Well, Zoe, why don't you give your letter to me. I'll hold it until Diego remembers where he is."

I nodded, bid her goodbye, and walked two blocks down to Dearborn Street, laughing all the way. Danny's address was 44 Dearborn Street. I didn't have to ring the bell there, either. Danny was waiting for me on his bike out front, and as soon as he saw me, he raced over, planning no doubt, to come to a screeching halt right in front of me.

"Hello, Zoe! Wait!" He shouted and tried to stop, turned too sharply and tumbled off his bike, bounced on his butt, and finally came to a skidding stop right in front of me. I know he wasn't faking it, you just can't plan something like that.

"Oh, hi Danny!" I greeted him. "So nice to run into you again, or should I say you ran into me? I need your help. Do you know where Julian and Josh live? I have something for them."

"Julian and Jo...? Wait, what?" He asked it with a hint of disappointment and I waited for his answer. "They live over there!" He pointed at the house across the street.

"Thanks!" I said and started to walk away, counting the steps in my mind. And before I reached five, Danny was right behind me: "Hey, uhh – what about me? Don't you have one of those for me?"

"Oh, sorry!" I said. "How silly of me! Here you go!" I held up the envelope with his name written on it. "And would you also like a Band-Aid for your butt?"

Danny blushed the color of my cleats, snatched the envelope from me and instantly ran away. You'll have to ask him why he left his bike behind. Boys are mysterious creatures.

Anyhoo, things went just as I'd planned and my desperation of the night before was a distant memory. But the moment I walked into Josh and Julian's backyard, the memory hit me like a lightning bolt.

Tyler, Fabio, and Kevin were waiting for me, along with Josh and Julian. The five of them stood there like garden gnomes, staring dumbly at me. Kevin pointed at the trashcan next to the driveway.

"You can put your letters right in there." His voice was harsh and mean.

"What are you waiting for?" Tyler added icily. Fabio spat, the way Kevin spat after I missed my last penalty shot, standing right above me, asking: "What do you think, Phooey? Did you pass the test?"

I didn't know what to do. I knew what I wanted to do – I wanted to run away. Then I wanted to throw the letters into the trashcan, like Kevin said. But I couldn't do that either. I promised my father the night before.

And so I dug up whatever courage I had left, and confronted Kevin. "Throw them in the trash yourself!" I snapped and looked him straight in the eye. "It's up to you. I don't mind. At least I'll know for sure – that you didn't have the guts to do this fair and square."

"You're the kind of girl who always thinks she's right," Roger worked up the courage to spit out.

I gave him my snake-eyes. "It's not about *who's* right. It's about *what's* right."

With that, I threw the letters at their feet, spun around, and marched away.

That night my dad and I sat in the living room on the new sofa that arrived couple of hours earlier. I had

no idea what was going to happen next. I usually know because I'm usually the one who messes things up. But I didn't do that this time. I was feeling oddly okay for the first time in a long time and when my father asked me how it went, I didn't hesitate. "Great, Dad," I said. "It went great."

"Were you scared much?" He asked.

"Oh yeah," I answered.

"Well, then you did the right thing by facing your fears," he said. "Gimme five."

I high-fived him and he laughed. "I'll bet you anything Kevin and the rest are shaking in their boots right now, staring at those envelopes, totally clueless."

I kissed him good night and went to bed. And that night I had the best sleep I've had in a long, long time. And that's how I knew I'd done something right.

Tremors in Camelot

My father was right. Larry had told him later that the *Wild Soccer Bunch* and he had gathered that night in Camelot, which was actually Julian's treehouse. The way he told it, they all stared at the eleven envelopes lying on an old wooden barrel right in front of them, unopened. They called it the anvil, and they only used it when a terrible danger was threatening them.

Dark expressions clouded their faces as they sat around the anvil staring down at the unopened letters. One of them looked like it had been opened and hastily resealed. The one with "Danny" written on it. That's why Danny wasn't looking at the envelopes. Instead, he squirmed and whistled *Knocking on Heaven's Door,* which is what he always did to push away the fear.

It was already dark when Kevin finally broke the silence. "Okay, we have two choices: burn them or open them."

"Burn them!" The words escaped Danny's mouth. "I vote we burn them."

Kevin looked at him and nodded in satisfaction. "What do you think?" he asked the others.

"Burn them."

"Yes, burn them."

"Let's burn them!" Everyone seemed to agree.

"And before we burn them, tear them to shreds."

Then everything was still.

Kevin waited a few seconds. "Good," sighed in relief. "It's settled then."

Slowly he bent down to the anvil to collect the letters. Larry watched him carefully, then started clapping slowly. "Very impressive, guys!" He said in mock praise. "And guess what? You look like real champions. But tell me one thing – does it hurt?"

Kevin balled his hands into a fist and Tyler squinted. Larry must have seen that; there was no way he could have missed it. But he didn't care. He took Danny's letter from the bunch and held it against the light.

"You guys beat the *Unbeatables,* you jump from a bridge in the middle of the night into scary water; an international soccer star is so impressed with you, he buys you your uniforms, and you call yourselves the *Wild Soccer Bunch.* That's quite a list of accomplishments. Until now. You get one little letter from a very nice girl who loves the game more than life itself – and you all turn into nervous Chihuahuas. Your fear beats you, and you're too wrapped up in yourselves to do anything about it."

"All right, that's enough!" Tyler and Kevin seethed.

Larry just looked at them like they were little kids.

"I'm not done yet," he said. "I have one question: Why didn't you do what Danny did?"

Danny shrunk back and tried to hide, but Larry stopped him. "Knock it off, Danny. Hiding doesn't become you. It so happens you were the only one brave enough to even *open* the letter. It doesn't matter if you did it for other reasons; at least you had the guts to do it. Maybe a little of that courage will rub off on your friends. Maybe they'll work up the nerve to read the letter before they stomp on it, tear it to shreds and torch it?" Larry cheered Danny on. But Danny just shook his head. "No, not in a million years. No way!"

Larry shook his head, disappointed. "It's that bad, huh? Wow. I guess I completely underestimated Zoe."

"You got that right," Danny said under his breath, and that's when Kevin couldn't stand it anymore. "I'm not underestimating and I'm not afraid!" he yelled, snatching the letter from Larry's hand and tearing open the envelope. A second later the letter was back on the anvil, now unfolded for everyone to read.

Hello Sweetie-pies!

Boy are you guys wild! At least that's what I thought, until I met you. You look pretty tough on the outside, but on the inside, you are just a bunch of chickens who know how to spit. You know, I would have thought that playing the game the way you do, you would have learned some manners, but I didn't see them out there on the field yesterday. Don't you agree, Roger? Diego? Alex? Kevin? Danny?

Well, it doesn't matter. I wouldn't expect you to take another look at me. After all, I'm just a girl and since you haven't figured out that we're humans too, I wouldn't expect you to give me another look. If you did, you might have to play by the rules and I don't think you guys know how to do that, let alone be fair.

Well, just the same, if you have a change of heart, you are cordially invited to my birthday party.

I am hosting a soccer tournament in my backyard at the Creepy Castle, 1 Old Sutton Road, at 3PM next Sunday, the day before school starts. Please come if you regain your sanity. And bring some manners. In my house, we don't treat people the way you treated me.

Otherwise, spit on the invitations or whatever you boys do with scary envelopes and I'll see you in P.E. when school starts. Have a nice day.

XOXOX,

Zoe

Silence fell over Camelot. But if you listened closely, you'd notice it was really loud. Loud as a Rolling Stones concert. Unbearably loud, to tell the truth, but in a frequency human ears cannot hear. The *Wild Soccer Bunch* could not hear the noise yet, but they could feel it. A thousand bats sent their calls out into the night and engulfed them. The ground shook and a tremor hit Camelot. The air was electrified with sparks of anger flying from one wild guy to the next. There was no need to utter a single word. They all knew. Finally the noise exploded when Kevin erupted, "She'll pay for this! I swear!"

Black Riders

The next morning the moving van finally showed up with my black mountain bike. Nothing else mattered any more, and much to Grandma's disdain – who had seriously hoped to have some girl talk with me and discuss how best to organize the kitchen shelves – I took off.

I rode without thinking. I didn't look right or left except when I came to corners. I just held my head high in the wind and raced through the streets. It felt good, and that's why I didn't see the danger lurking at every corner. They were dressed all in black, their faces hidden behind black hoods. I didn't notice them until three of them were right behind me and I could hear the whirr of their mountain bikes on the asphalt. They were chasing me! When I looked back I saw their black hoodies and the black *Wild Soccer Bunch* signs on their handles. Boys. What is wrong with their brains? I sped up. I rode as fast as I could, trying to lose them, but they stuck to me like a shadow. My only chance was to head for home immediately. "Take the next left and then turn left again," I thought, but I wasn't quite sure because I didn't really know my way around yet. But the fourth hunter was waiting for me at the corner, and number 5 was straight ahead, so all I could do was turn right. I had no idea where that street would lead, but I took it anyway. "Take the next right," I thought, "then straight home." But that wasn't in the cards.

At the next corner, and the next one, and the one after that, more black riders appeared, and they chased me through strange streets right into the "The Garden," a bike park. There, the last of the eleven Black Riders was waiting for me. They surrounded me like sharks in a feeding frenzy and no matter what I tried or how many neck-breaking tricks I dared, I couldn't shake them. Every time I made a maneuver, one of the black riders would appear right in front of me, blocking my escape, and finally, even my one advantage – my fat back tire – didn't help any more. I lost my balance and tumbled down the embankment.

I jumped up immediately, but my bike was stuck underneath a tree trunk. I pulled and tugged, but I couldn't get it out. Oh no! I panicked, when they all caught up and surrounded me. But before I could scream, they ripped off their hoods.

"Get outta town! She's got a Mongoose!" Roger yelled.

"Yeah, and you see that back tire?" Tyler added. "You won't even slip on ice with that one! Awesome!"

But Kevin held up his hand, demanding silence. "Not bad," he said dryly. "Really, I mean it. But it doesn't quite cut it."

I stared at him. "You think eleven against one cuts it? You are more pathetic than I thought," I said.

Kevin's face twitched for a few seconds. He couldn't

hide behind a glob of spit that time.

"Okay!" he said and smiled gracefully. "We're all looking forward to your soccer tournament."

It took me a second to process this. "Hold on. Are you saying you're going to show up?" I asked. "You're really going to come?"

"Can a chicken spit?" Kevin shot me a knowing glance and I had to stifle a laugh.

"We even bought you a birthday present, Phooey!" Kevin grinned, pulled a back-wheelie and turned around. A loud battle cry on his lips, he took the ramp and raced off. The others followed, easily navigating the hills and ramps of the park.

I couldn't hold it in any longer. "IT'S ZOE!!" I yelled at the top of my lungs. Every single last one of the *Wild Soccer Bunch* stopped and looked back. Even Kevin, Tyler, and Danny, who had already climbed the embankment above me, turned their bikes as if they were ponies and looked down upon me like a band of Indian warriors.

I launched my bike, took the next three ramps fast and without stopping, and then I turned my bike around in a wheelie. For a brief sweet moment, I savored the stunned looks of the *Wild Soccer Bunch*. Then I calmly said, "I'm looking forward to the party, too. See you Sunday."

With a last glance at Kevin, Tyler, and Danny, I wheelied my bike like a horse and took off back down the hill leaving them in my dust. I felt fantastic. Lucky for me I didn't turn around to see Kevin sitting on top of the embankment like a king on his throne. "I can't wait," he hissed. "This is not over yet."

Dead Center and Right in the Heart

It was pouring rain that Sunday morning. When I came into the kitchen, Grandma was about to decorate my birthday cake with pink frosting. "What do you think your new girlfriends would like to drink?" she asked. "Cocoa or tea?"

"Girlfriends?" I asked and looked at my father in confusion. He just shrugged. "I told her who was coming, but she didn't believe me."

Grandma didn't seem to hear him. "And what have you planned after the cake? At first I was thinking a little hide-and-seek or maybe a sack race? But since it's raining we'll have to play indoor games."

"Indoor games? Grandma, are you kidding me?" I repeated and sat down at the table. "How about spin-the-bottle?"

Grandma, mortified, dropped the frosting. "Oh dear, dear, dear, child! Don't you think you're a little young for that?"

"Yes, Grandma, I'm just kidding! I don't know if you noticed or not, but I don't have any girlfriends here in Chicago. Just boys," I explained, grinning sheepishly. "So, I only invited boys."

"And whether they're friends remains to be seen," my father chimed in.

I nodded agreement with dad as Grandma was lost in her shock.

"Boys?" Grandma repeated in horror. "Spin-the-bottle? Scott-Francis, did you have anything to do with this? She's too young!"

"Don't get all jiggy, Grandma," I said. "We're having a soccer tournament. In the backyard."

At first she looked relieved, then realized what I'd just said. "Wait a minute. Outside? In the rain?" Grandma plopped down in her chair.

"Sure! In the rain. Soccer doesn't mind the rain and neither do I!" I said, taking another look at her pink cake. "Oh, would you please change the color of the frosting? I want black."

"Black?" She said, flabbergasted. "Why in heaven's name would you want black?"

I grinned. "It's the team colors of the *Wild Soccer Bunch*."

Grandma could only mouth the words and watch

dumbfounded as I rushed out to get ready.

And when she threw open the front door at 3 p.m. sharp to greet the *Wild Soccer Bunch* on our doorstep, she was speechless. The whole team arrived on their bikes, all clad in black. They didn't even notice the rain and they cared even less about the dirt on their pants and hoodies and faces. "The *Wild Soccer Bunch*, I presume," was all she said.

Despite her sincere desire for a little girl tea-and-crumpets dress-up birthday party for her only granddaughter, Grandma knew this was not going to be it. This was going to be a battle: a battle between lofty dreams and old beliefs. A battle between a girl dreaming to go all the way to the U.S. National Soccer Team, and eleven wildly determined boys who believe that a girl's place is in the playhouse and the beauty parlor, not on the soccer field. Now *that* is a contest.

"Did you kids just crawl out from under a rock?" Grandma lamented, looking at each of the boys as if they just stepped out of a mud bath.

"I wish," Kevin said and the rest of the guys laughed. "We'll meet you around the back, Phooey" he said as he spun his bike like a wild bronco and tore off for the side gate, followed by the rest of the *Wild Soccer Bunch*.

"Phooey?"

"Grandma, you are so uptight," I said, closing the front door. "They're shy. Cut them some slack. For now."

"I get it, the strong and silent types eh?"

"Well, I don't know about that," I replied.

"Okay. Well, what do we do now? I admit I'm totally at a loss."

"What do you think? First we eat cake – and then we fight."

"Fight?"

"Yes, Grandma, fight, the way you fought Muhammad Ali," I explained and pulled her into the kitchen to get the cake.

"What does Muhammad Ali have to do with the tea in China?" Grandma asked, trying to figure out what the heck I was talking about.

"Grandma, did you or did you not want to become a heavyweight champion once upon a time?"

Grandma blushed. It was the first time I'd ever seen her do that and at first I thought something was wrong, but she immediately said: "I was just a kid, then," Grandma hesitated. "I didn't know any better."

"Well, now you do," I said. "Besides, you're the only woman here. I need you to remember!"

"Remember what?"

"Remember everything I'm not supposed to do!" I said impatiently, pushing one of the black soccer ball birthday cakes into her hand. Then I took the other one and returned to my dark and sinister guests.

They were amazed when they saw the two black soccer ball birthday cakes. And they were so sure of their victory that they ate every last crumb. Roger even ate five pieces all by himself, and with each piece his mood seemed to lighten. And his mood was contagious; he was telling jokes, and he even told Grandma about Mickey the Bulldozer and his slob friends the *Unbeatables,* and how they'd beat them in a match. It almost felt like a *real* birthday party.

Then my father explained the rules. You'll play two on two, in six teams and two groups. In each group the teams will oppose each other twice to decide the semi-finalists. In the semi-finals, the winner of Group One will meet the runner-up of Group Two and the other way around. The winners of these games will meet in the finals.

"Got it," Kevin said dryly. "But who plays with her?" He pointed at me. "Except for Grandma, I don't see any other girls. And the way I see it, Grandma's not only too old, but she's also too pink."

"Old enough to teach *you* a thing or two, young man!" Grandma grumbled and pointed a finger at them and they backed up. My father stepped in, "There are eleven of you, right? Depending on the way you look at it, there is either one too many or one too few. Either way, one of you is going to play with Zoe. Who is it going to be?"

"Good question," Kevin shrugged and addressed his team in disbelief. "Any volunteers?"

Danny was about to raise his hand when Kevin slapped it down.

"What's the matter with you? You're on my team!" Kevin knew Danny was a little different than the others and had a crush on me. "Tyler plays with the girl," Kevin decided, and put me with the one wild guy who disliked me as much as he did.

"I'm not 'the girl,' Kevin. My name is Zoe."

"Right," he said, shooting a quick look to my father. "We have something for your daughter," Kevin said as if my name was unmentionable. "We bought her a present, and I'd like to give it to her now."

With that, he magically produced a pink package from his black backpack and gave it to me. "Thank you for that very sweet letter. We bought this just for you," he said earnestly. "So you never forget who you are."

My mouth was glued shut and all I could do was nod. I had a bad feeling about this.

I opened the package anyway. If you've learned anything about me you already know I live dangerously... and wild. I pulled on the pink ribbon, ripped off the pink wrapping paper and found a pink shoe box inside. "You sure you want me to open this now?" I managed to ask Kevin with a slight quaver in my voice.

"Please," he said. "Unless you don't have the guts."

My stomach knotted up. But my mom and dad taught me that everything has consequences, and I guess that includes letters to the *Wild Soccer Bunch*. I prepared myself for a dose of my own medicine, then slowly removed the lid from the shoebox. What I found inside hit me dead center, right in the heart. Talk about mean! Even Grandma gasped. Inside the box was a pair of pink high heels with rhinestones and flowers. I was speechless. I wanted to throw Kevin to the ground. Maybe my father saw my body language or something because he suddenly jumped in front of me and said, "Why don't you go out back and start the tournament?"

I glared at Kevin and let the box drop to the floor, and then I turned on my heel and stomped out.

A Question of Honor

The field was sixteen yards long and nine yards wide, the maximum our backyard would allow. My father drew the lines with chalk like a real pro and put up practice goals. The 'last man' would be the goalie, each game would be five minutes long and the host team – Tyler and myself – was up first.

The rain was still coming down pretty good and the ground was slippery and my knees were trembling. I tried to forget the pink high heels, but they were stuck in my head like a bad song I couldn't get rid of. What if everyone was right – Grandma and Kevin and Fabio and Tyler? What if a girl really had no business being on the same team with the *Wild Soccer Bunch?* What if I lose today? All these negative thoughts kept shooting around inside my head and fear grabbed me by the throat. I didn't have a chance. That was crystal clear the minute my opponents, Danny and Kevin, stepped out on the field. They were so sure of their victory; I could see it in their faces and every move they made. I looked to Tyler

for help, but what was the point of that? I was all alone out there. Tyler didn't even try to hide his indifference. It was clear, he wasn't going to lift a finger for me. And guess what? I was right. It only took seven seconds for Danny to pass to Kevin, because Tyler looked the other way. And I looked like an amateur as Kevin faked me out. I fell flat on my butt and, sitting there in the mud, I watched Kevin easily push the ball over the goal line.

During the counterattack I passed the ball to Tyler, but he skidded past the ball, plopped himself into the mud and watched as Kevin and Danny out-played me with a double pass.

At two-zero, the two of them slowed down, because they could. My knees were like jell-o and Tyler acted as if he'd never played before. Kevin and Danny destroyed us, and I was lucky the game ended at five-zero. It could have been worse.

In the other group, Fabio and Diego beat Roger and Alex with a tight match ending two-one. The next game, Kevin and Danny versus Josh and Julian, was important. If Julian and Josh lost, Tyler and I had a chance to get into second place. But Kevin and Danny played so badly it was as if they were someone else, and the game ended in a tie. Now it was our turn to beat Julian and Josh, but once again, Tyler did his best to play lousy, and I was lucky to eke out a tie in the last minute. I was exactly where the *Wild Soccer Bunch* wanted me: bringing up the rear with only a solitary goal.

I had lost all my courage and confidence and wanted to run to my father for help. But when I looked at him and he looked at me, I knew I had to do this myself. But how? I watched the games of the other teams carefully, trying to figure out what to do. Their games were different. They played the way I wanted everyone to play in my birthday soccer tournament. They fought hard. They took it seriously. No one smiled at anyone else, and in the end all three teams, Fabio and Diego, Joey and Kyle, and Alex and Roger had tied in points and goals. I have to admit, it was a lot of fun to watch and it made me forget the mess I was in. But then Kevin and Danny waited for me again, and Tyler still moved around on the field like he had two left feet. One-zero against us was only a matter of time and I could feel the anger growing inside of me and it pushed out all my fears. I was ready for them and boy did I turn it on. I zooted Tyler out of frame and played by myself. I managed to tie, but then Tyler, the coward, handed the lead back to them by scoring into our own goal. That's when I lost it.

"Are you kidding me?! You're gonna let us lose that way, you pitiful wimp?" I yelled. "Where's your sense of honor?"

Tyler blushed. I could see he was embarrassed, but he couldn't get out from under the peer pressure of the rest of his teammates. Kevin and Danny scored one more goal and we left the field with a three-one loss. We were still ranked last.

The game matching Danny and Kevin with Josh and Julian would decide if I'd have a chance to make the semi-finals. But Kevin didn't even consider giving me a chance. Even a loss would leave his team in first place – he had planned it that way – and Josh and Julian were supposed to stay in second place. That's why he didn't do anything. He played so badly even Danny was embarrassed. When Josh, tiny little Josh, scored a goal right through Kevin's legs, Danny lost his temper. He grabbed the ball, raced up to the other side of the field and thundered the ball into the net.

"Hey! What are you doing?" Kevin screamed. "Are you nuts?"

"No, but I think you are. And I think what you're doing sucks!"

"Oh yeah?" Kevin hissed. "And all you want to do is let her win. I think you're crushing on her!"

Danny blushed. He was embarrassed. But unlike Tyler he shook off the peer pressure.

"So what?" he stammered. "I still want to win fair

and square. And this ain't fair."

At that moment my father whistled. Their game ended in a tie. And that's how my team suddenly had a shot at second place. All we had to do was win against Josh and Julian. "Did you hear that?" I asked Tyler, trembling all over.

Tyler didn't say a word. Not even a nod. But I wasn't going to let him off the hook that easily. I summoned up all my courage and got in his face and cut to the chase: "Okay, I'm begging you – give me a chance. You'd do it if I was a boy."

I waited, biting my lip. Finally Tyler looked at me one last time, then moved out. He ran onto the field, took the ball and when he noticed that I wasn't right behind him, he turned and said: "What are you waiting for? I can't do this by myself!"

My heart thumped like a bass drum. I beamed. Oh, did I beam. I beamed through the whole game because it was so much fun. Tyler showed how well he played and I finally had a chance to show my soccer chops as well. Julian fought like a lion and even six-year-old Josh played better than his years, but in the end it wasn't enough and we won three-two.

"Wow!" I was thrilled. Tyler gave me a high five. We had made the semifinals! Even Kevin's sour face couldn't change that. He approached Fabio and Diego who had scored first in their group.

"Can I count on you to beat her?" he asked.

"Like taking candy from a baby," Fabio promised, every one of his pores oozing confidence.

Sweet Revenge

Before Fabio could keep his promise, the other semifinal took place. Kevin and Danny worked it against Joey and Kyle. This game was like a powder keg about to explode.

Kevin loathed Danny, his best friend; loathed him with a passion. Danny humiliated him in front of everyone, and on top of that, he paved the way to the semifinals for me. The air between them was thicker than honey, and because you can't really play in honey, Joey and Kyle were in the lead. It was two-nothing in less than a minute, and every mistake Kevin made, he blamed Danny. In the end, Kevin was the only one playing, and Danny just angrily went through the motions. He yelled at Kevin who yelled right back, and by the time it was four-nothing, the two of them were fighting in the mud.

"You didn't pass to me!" Danny yelled, pushing Kevin on his back and sitting on top of him.

"You got that right!" Kevin yelled back, pushing

Danny's face down into the grass and twisting his arm. "You like her, don't you! You want her to win!"

"Really? Take it back!" Danny hissed and tried to lift his face out of the mud. "Who's the biggest loser now?"

Kevin gritted his teeth and got in Danny's face. "You are. To me."

"Great and how's *that* going to help the team? We're just helping *her*."

"No way!" Kevin hissed and put Danny in an arm-lock.

"We can't beat her, dude!" Danny grimaced. "You really think I'd lose a tournament on purpose? No girl's worth losing a game over! I wasn't faking it. I couldn't beat her!"

"No way!"

"Yes, way!" Danny shot back. "Now get off me!"

"Hurry!" My father shouted. "You have 90 seconds left on the clock!"

That's when the game turned. Danny and Kevin made peace with each other. They were the 'Lightning Duo,' as if Leo Messi and Cristiano Ronaldo played on the same team. In the final second and a half of the game, Danny passed brilliantly to Kevin who gracefully lifted the ball into the net to the tune of a four-four tie.

It was time for penalty kicks. Kyle marched into the goal against Kevin and Danny. But with all due respect for Kyle's natural talent and invincible as he was, he didn't stand a chance against Danny and Kevin. The two of them thundered the balls into the net so hard that after a while, Kyle didn't even *try* to hold them anymore.

Danny and Kevin definitely deserved their spot in the final. I hated to admit it because it was hard getting motivated against them, but the truth was, they played very well. The way they worked together, no one could beat them. I knew that, so what was the point of winning against Diego and Fabio in our semifinal? The only thing I'd get was facing Kevin in the finals. Oh, I could see it, as if it had happened already, as if I was watching it on instant replay. Kevin would come right up to me, puff himself up, and look at me with contempt. Then he'd utter those lethal words. "Not bad,

Phooey. But not good enough." And then he and his *Wild Soccer Bunch* would disappear from my life forever.

That's what I was thinking and I probably would have been thinking it for the rest of my life if Tyler hadn't woken me up. "Hey, Zoe! Fabio is right in front of you and he's ready to keep his promise."

I looked at Tyler blankly.

"Hello? He wants to beat us?" Tyler grinned.

"I will beat you, because I always keep my promises," Fabio responded. "No matter how well she plays, the girl always loses. Remember that."

I believed every word he said, but Tyler just laughed. "Well, I guess that means you're a girl. Because you're going to lose."

Fabio fumed and it intimidated me, but Tyler's humor encouraged me.

So, every time Fabio crossed my path, I thought, *Fabio's a girl.* It worked! My fear left me and the game was a nail biter. One minute before the final whistle, Diego scored one-zero after he charged forward dribbling the ball as heavenly as only he can. Fabio was playing brilliantly. But Tyler didn't give up, and that was the only asset we needed. He split right into one of Fabio's attempts at a score against us, pushed it through his legs, and past Diego into the goal. Wow! That was something! And then Tyler did it a second time. Ten seconds before the final whistle he lifted the ball with his ankle and pushed it into the net high above Fabio and Diego's heads. That was our victory goal. I couldn't believe it. What a day! Half an hour ago Tyler hated me with a passion, and now he'd won our semifinal – for me.

Then things got even better. Grandma came running from the kitchen into the rain and hugged Tyler, "Oh dear, dear, dear, you have made me so happy!"

Tyler, being squeezed by Grandma, looked to me for help, but I made it clear he was on his own, and so he wound up doing his best to hide his embarrassment.

Fabio, in the meantime, had snuck off the field and crawled up to Kevin like an wounded tiger and hissed. "She's a sorcerer! Just look at the house. It's like some haunted castle. Kevin, I'm warning you, you better watch out!" Fabio was dazed and confused and looked as if he wanted to wear a garlic necklace, but Kevin just pushed him harder.

"You're talking crazy, Fabio," Kevin said. "Besides – the girl didn't beat you, Tyler did. Why wouldn't he? He's playing awesome today!" Kevin said it with as much contempt as he could muster. "Tyler is a pest, but don't worry. Our time is coming. He can play as great as he wants – he's not going to beat Danny and me."

"Yeah, but what about – Zoe?" Fabio asked.

"Don't tell me you're worried about *the girl?*"

"*I'm* not worried, Kevin. But *you* should be!"

Kevin rolled his eyes. "Come on, Danny! Fabio doesn't get it. Let's put the *real* world back together."

With that, Kevin and Danny lined up on the field, cheered on by the *Wild Soccer Bunch*. Tyler and I on the other hand, had only a solitary fan. But I wouldn't trade this fan for a thousand of theirs.

"Go get 'em! Knock 'em dead. Shoot 'em to the moon!

And make sure they don't come back!" Grandma stood on the sidelines yelling and jumping up and down like a banshee.

My father blew the whistle. The finals had begun. Neither team showed any mercy. Every one of us ended up in the dirt rolling in pain more than once, but none of us slowed down. Instead, the pain motivated us. In the third minute of the game, Danny thundered a ball towards one corner of our goal, but Tyler diverted it by a touch of his magic fingertips. Then I took a shot three feet from the goal aiming at the lower right-hand corner. But at the very last second Kevin dove down like a dolphin and derailed the ball around the goal post. Attack followed attack and the game was almost over. There were mere seconds left on the clock when Danny shot the ball over Tyler's head into our penalty box. That's where Kevin was making a run. This was his kingdom. But the pass was too high and he couldn't reach the ball. The danger had passed. I breathed a sigh of relief, when suddenly Kevin turned, his legs flew in the air and, with a bicycle kick, sent the ball towards the net. I winced and rushed to the right. I flew through the air and stretched as far as I could, and, cheered on by Grandma, I fisted the ball back onto the field. That's where Tyler plucked it right out of the air and pushed it further towards the opponent's goal. The goal was empty. Nobody could have stopped the shot, and the ball was a dive bomber screaming toward the goal. "Goal!" Grandma yelled and covered her face in her hands. That's when the ball hit the goal post and went out of bounds just as my father blew the final whistle.

Regulation time was over, and penalty kicks would decide the game. That was exactly what I wanted to avoid at all cost. In the semifinal, Danny and Kevin proved they were unbeatable. I, on the other hand, failed miserably during practice. Now what? This was exactly what I didn't want, so I asked Tyler to take all our penalty shots. He declined. Instead, he asked even more of me. He wanted me to be our goalie.

"No way!" I refused, but Tyler just shrugged, an expression he probably learned from Larry the coach.

"Fine, but don't come whining to me when they say it was me who beat them, not you," he said calmly. And then he smiled as only he can smile. Oh, how I learned to hate that smile. But I couldn't resist it. I stopped moping and marched into our goal.

Kevin was up first. He put the ball down just so, and then took three steps back and mercilessly hammered it into the upper right-hand corner. I didn't even move.

I was up next.

Of course, Kevin went to cover the goal. I closed my eyes, cursed all my past mistakes, and charged, drenched in insecurity. I feinted to the left and then kicked the ball towards the lower right-hand corner. This time it would work! But no, Kevin was right there even before the ball and caught it easily.

"Is that all you've got?" he grinned as he passed me, leisurely jogging out of the goal. "That one didn't work in practice, either."

I had had it. But Tyler wouldn't let me give up. "If you hold this next one, I promise, we'll win." His voice could have convinced me that two and two were five and a half. I dutifully marched back into the goal, ready for Danny's penalty kick. Oh, Danny was so sure of his victory. Not a tinge of doubt in his eyes. Not even for a moment did he consider thinking that he could fail. Bursting with that confidence, he charged the ball and pulled the trigger. I watched the ball approach, but I didn't react. I just ducked a little as the ball bounced off the crossbar and back out into the field. And just like that we were back in the game!

Tyler took the next shot. He didn't charge. That is, he hesitated for a second, waiting for Kevin to choose a corner, and then he leisurely aimed his shot at the opposite corner and BLAM! It was a one-one tie.

Kevin was steamed and now he had to let Danny go first. Sudden death was in play, and from that point on, every missed penalty kick could mean losing the game.

Danny knew that, too, and he had learned his lesson from his arrogant first shot. This time he focused everything he had and charged and cut it loose. He didn't risk a thing and trusted the power of his shot. But I guessed the corner and dove for it with everything in me. I stretched further than I'd ever stretched before and touched the ball with my fingertips. But the shot was too hard. It flew over the goal line and landed in the net. Kevin and Danny were in the lead again and if Tyler missed his next shot, I would lose everything.

But Tyler was cool. This time he charged. He didn't play any tricks, just smacked the ball short and hard into the corner. Two-two. Now it was all up to Kevin and me.

I tried to convince Tyler one more time to goalie for me, but as usual, he declined again. "What's the matter?" he asked. "You almost held Danny's ball. Just imagine what Kevin will do if you hold *his* shot." And what he said next, delivered with his signature smile, made all the difference. "Come on, I know you can do it."

Ten seconds later, Kevin placed the ball on the penalty spot. Then he charged. I tried to guess the corner. Upper-right again? Or lower-left, like any other right-footed player when he is nervous? Is Kevin nervous? I didn't think so, and that's why even before he took his shot, I dove towards the upper right-hand corner.

I put all my eggs in one basket and, what do you know – I was right! I triumphantly fisted the ball out into the field.

Kevin was frozen. He couldn't believe it. Nobody could believe it. Even Grandma was speechless. No, wait a minute, no wonder she was so quiet. She wasn't there anymore. Where did she go? Did she give up on me? I kept telling myself to get out of my head and into the game. Come on, I thought to myself, I had held the penalty kick and now everything was in my hands. I

could win the tournament all by myself, the way Tyler had planned. I looked over at him and he nodded back to me. I could see he was nervous too. He wasn't just biting his lip – he was *chewing* it!

Nervous and insecure, I placed the ball on the penalty spot. I trembled. I stepped back to charge, and that's when the memory of everything you *shouldn't* remember, came flooding back into my brain. I remembered the practice and lived through it one more time, blow-by-blow. I slipped in the mud. Kevin appeared above me and grinned, contempt written all over his face. Once again, he made his snide and hurtful comment, "What do you think, Phooey? Did you pass the test?"

I couldn't see the goal any more. All I saw was a gigantic version of Kevin, guarding it. How would I ever get a ball past him?

I was just about to charge, every muscle in my body locked into place, when suddenly my Grandma came loping in front of me. "You should wear these for the winning kick." She was holding the pink high heels. "So you'll remember who you are. Remember? Isn't that what he said? Go for it, tiger, show him what you got."

I thought about it. My mind boggled. Everyone was staring at me waiting to do something. Kevin wasn't sure what was going on. I made my decision, then

plopped down where I stood, tore off my cleats, and
quickly pulled on the pink high heels. They were two
sizes too big.

I wobbled in the heels over to the penalty spot, put

the ball exactly where I wanted it, and took aim. Kevin
tried to look cool, but I saw in his eyes that the sight
of those pink high heels freaked him out as he got ready
for my shot.

I knew exactly what I was doing. I charged, feinted to

the left and with the outside of my heels, now covered in glorious hardened mud, I kicked... and the ball sailed... and sailed... and seemed to soar forever. Kevin dove left and I nailed it into the right corner. SCORE!

I did it! I must have jumped three feet in the air and screamed for joy. I won my birthday soccer tournament in pink high heels! How delicious was that! I had shown the *Wild Soccer Bunch* who I really was! I ran over to Grandma and grabbed her hands and danced around in the rain until we were dizzy. Then I hugged my father and kissed him on the cheek. And then I stood right in front of Tyler, who took a few steps back, just in case my enthusiasm got the best of me. "Thank you!" I said, beaming at him.

But there was something about Tyler's face. He didn't look like a winner at all. He took another step back. "No problem," he said hesitantly. "I gotta go."

And that's when I realized that he was the only one left. The rest of the *Wild Soccer Bunch* was gone. It was as if the ground had swallowed them up.

Revenge May Be Sweet, But It's Lonely

I watched as Tyler picked up his bike and disappeared from the yard. Then I helped my father and Grandma clean up. Quietly we cleaned up the yard and the kitchen, and when we were done, everyone went looking for a place to be by themselves. Every one of us had to think about what had just happened. Grandma was tortured by her conscience because she felt she ruined my birthday party. My father knew that he had to keep his promise and talk about going back to Somerville. And I went to my room to mope.

"It's lonely at the top," I thought to myself. Sure, I had shown Kevin and the *Wild Soccer Bunch*. I had beaten them and I had proved I was as good a player as they were. So why did I feel so lousy? What good did it do me? Vengeance was sweet, but I was all alone. I had won the tournament and lost the team. Did I go too far with the pink high heels? Maybe that had been just too humiliating for the *Wild Soccer Bunch* to take. My dream to be one of them had popped like a soap bubble. Then I realized, oh no – summer break was over tomorrow and I'd see them again at school. In fact, I'd see them every day. How was I going to face them? Even though I was a pretty grown up nine-year-old, it felt too much for me. The only thing I could do was move back to Somerville, preferably tonight and in a hurry. My father promised, more or less. But as much as I wanted to go back, I didn't feel right about that either.

There was a knock on my door and Grandma came in. "Oh, what a day!" She sighed and sat down on the mattress next to me. "Had I known, I would have stayed at home. I'm too old for this!" She gave me a glance and when she saw how desperate I was, she flashed me a smile.

I'd never seen that kind of a smile from her before. "Why are you smiling?" I asked.

She nodded. "I learned this smile from you, Zoe."

"Me?" I said.

"I saw it today out there on the field."

I was confused. Her smile was bright and wonderful. How could I have given her a bright and wonderful smile when everything was sad and desperate?

"I hope you don't think this means I'm going to suddenly start liking pink and acting like a little girl,"

I said.

"I did yesterday, but not today," she said.

"I'm always going to be me, Grandma," I said. "I am who I am."

"And I suppose you won't even *consider* a different sport."

I shrugged and shook my head.

"Oh dear, dear, dear, soccer is such a tough game. If I had known, I would have gotten thicker armor!"

The smile crept onto her face again and she took me gently into her arms. "And about those pink high heels, don't even think about them. Payback is a pain and now those boys know exactly who you are. You're not just a soccer girl who plays as well as they do."

"I'm not?"

"You're also... wild."

I fought a smile. Grandma hugged me hard and for the first time, I knew just how wonderful she was. When I closed my eyes, my mom was hugging me, too. I started feeling normal again. She smiled once more, and this time it was contagious. I couldn't resist and gave her my bright and wonderful smile. And we were both smiling like Cheshire cats when my father stormed into the room.

He didn't even knock and he had a dark expression on his face. He marched in and started throwing my stuff into a big suitcase.

"What are you doing?" I asked.

"Packing!" he grumbled.

"Packing? What on earth for?" Grandma asked and winked at me.

"We're going back to Somerville. Tonight," he grumbled on.

"Somerville? Why?" I said, winking back at Grandma.

"You're kidding me, right?" My father said, stopping. "You want to go back. I've already found a realtor for the house."

"Um, dad?" I murmured.

"Yes, tiger, I'm really busy, what is it?" he asked, continuing to throw stuff into the suitcase.

"I thought we were going to talk about it first."

"Well, yes, but I assumed it was settled so I made a decision for the both of us."

"I don't want to go back," I blurted out.

My father stopped packing. I couldn't tell what he was thinking, but when he looked at me, I knew immediately. It was that look he always gave me to let me know we were a team. "Mom knew this move would be good for us," I continued. "Well, guess what? She was right. This is our home now."

Grandma looked at us with teary eyes.

Then my father got all mushy-eyed too. "That's the nicest thing I've heard in a long time, tiger," he said.

"Dad, we make a great team and besides, I don't even remember where Somerville is."

My father pushed the suitcase aside, sat down beside me, put his arm around me, and squeezed me tight. "What about tomorrow?"

"Tomorrow," I said. "I'm getting up bright and early and I'm going to my new school. I hear it is going to be a beautiful day."

My dad smiled. "I heard the same thing."

I Am Who I Am

The next day I rode my bike to school. I was right. It was a beautiful fall day, all nice and warm, but I still pulled my hoodie up and hid deep inside it, because that's what I do when I'm determined and insecure at the same time. That's probably why I didn't see the slob until he was right in front of me. I had just locked my bike to a bike rack and was on my way to the school yard, when he suddenly appeared right in front of me and there was another guy right behind him. The front guy was mighty and fat, and his tiny beady eyes sat like black coals between his beefy cheeks. He wore a Darth Vader t-shirt, and his breath rattled like an elephant seal just coming up for air. Or did the rattle come from the bicycle chain the moron behind him was swinging in his hands?

Oh no, I thought. And I thought the *Wild Soccer Bunch* was mean.

"Well, well, well, what have we here?" The guy in the Darth Vader t-shirt snorted. "Looks like a sheep in wolf's clothing."

"I don't see any sheep,"
the boy with the bicycle
chain behind him said and
the Darth Vader
t-shirt smacked him
one on the back
of his head. "A
girl dressed up like
a boy," he said.

"Oh yeah," said bicycle
chain boy.

"A kitty cat playing a tiger,"
Darth Vader t-shirt continued.
"Boo!" He pushed the hoodie off my head. "Not only a
new cat, she's cute too."

"I'm cute enough if you're ugly enough," I countered
as calmly and icily as possible.

"You need glasses, girlfriend!" he spat onto the
cobblestones and got some of it on his shoe. He quickly
tried to hide it, but I was looking at it and he was
looking at it and when we both looked up at the same
time, our eyes met and he knew I'd seen the whole
thing. So he cleared his throat to move on with his
little drama but I interrupted him.

"What do you want, I gotta get to class," I said and tried to leave and they blocked my path again.

"We usually ask for a contribution from all the new students. You know," Darth Vader t-shirt said.

"Cash," bicycle chain guy said, trying to be ominous.

"But this is your lucky day," Darth Vader t-shirt continued. "I'm going to make an exception with you."

"Gee, what did I do to deserve this?" I asked.

"I'm Robin Hood. And I'll let you pass. For a kiss."

"A kiss," I repeated, dripping with sarcasm, shaking my head, chuckling to myself. "How about I just say 'good boy' and pet you. And I'll bet your pal with the oversized doggie tags wants one too, dontcha boy?!"

"That's a bicycle chain!" Darth Vader t-shirt threatened and snapped his fingers, and in no time more morons appeared at his side like flies on a day-old cheeseburger. There were at least seven of them now, and each one of them would fit perfectly into a bad horror movie. I was totally outnumbered.

As I expected, Darth Vader t-shirt made his move and like a monster, stomped towards me, his merry band of morons following right behind. I had only one defense left: empty threats and hope against hope that their collective IQ wasn't high enough to figure me out. I wasn't worried about Darth Vader t-shirt's big brain.

But how was I going to come up with an effective counter-threat when my life and limb were in danger? Besides, no one survives a kiss from Darth Vader.

"Dude, I'm warning you!" I hissed. "Don't touch me." Lame, I thought instantly. I braced for the worst, balled my hands into fists of fury and repeated, "This is your last warning, dude. Touch me – and I turn *you* into a girl!" While they were busy realizing I had just threatened them with a fate worse than detention, a miracle occurred.

Darth Vader t-shirt and his merry band of morons saw something behind me that I didn't and started backing away like old men, yelling, "This is not over, girlfriend! We'll meet again. Bet on it." Then they turned and stomped away.

I stared at my hands in disbelief. "Impossible!"

"No, it's totally possible," a voice behind me said matter of factly. "Welcome to school. I see you already met Mickey the bulldozer and the *Unbeatables*."

I turned around and there was Kevin, standing steadfast behind me, along with the rest of the *Wild Soccer Bunch*.

No wonder they turned and ran like a band of fat bunny rabbits.

"Thanks," I said, relieved, but Kevin didn't say another word. He just shyly nodded; so Tyler kicked him in the shin.

"Ah, don't mention it!" Kevin blurted out in pain. "No need to thank us! Now you know there are worse things than the *Wild Soccer Bunch*."

That said, he wanted to turn around and leave, but Danny stopped him. "Kevin, aren't you forgetting something?"

"Am I? Oh, yeah, right. Well, I don't know," he stammered, and Tyler kicked him in the shin again.

"Ouch! Are you nuts, that's my kicking foot! Okay, okay, let me talk, will you?!" he complained and pulled a white package from his black backpack.

"Here," he said and held it under my nose. "I guess this evens the score."

Surprised, I took the package, and Kevin limped away,

miffed. Three steps later he turned around and said: "Oh, and just so you know. Even though you're just a girl, I have to admit... you are... really wild!" And for the first time in a long time, he grinned. I could hardly believe it. Then he limped off. It was the nicest thing he'd ever said to me.

The others stayed and formed a circle around me. Slowly, I opened the white wrapping paper and took out something black and soft. I unfolded it and stared at it in disbelief. It was a new *Wild Soccer Bunch* jersey, with the number 5 on it, and the words *Wild Soccer Bunch* underneath. And above that, it said:

Zoe the fearless.

The *Wild Soccer Bunch*

Well folks, that's my story and I'm sticking to it. I finally made it. Imagine this: I, Zoe the fearless, was now part of the *Wild Soccer Bunch*. I felt like I'd just been knighted by King Arthur. Camelot was not just a place I read about in fairy tales, it was a tree house where the *Wild Soccer Bunch* meets. And plans things. Together. It was where they decided to let me join the team. I knew at that precise moment, as sure as I'd ever been, that I'd play for the U.S. National Soccer Team and considering how well the women's' team is doing, I just might play for them. I mean, a girls' team is only as good as its players, right?

Well, Grandma told me that I could be the one who could bring greatness to any team, so why not? And because that's how it went down, I have some time for you now. But what is it you wanted again? Oh, right, I was supposed to tell you about the *Wild Soccer Bunch*. Well, now that I know them a little bit better, I don't really know where to start.

Let's see... sure why not. So, one of them is called Danny. He is the world's fastest right forward and the wildest of the bunch. And that's the truth. I'll tell you, he's already interested in girls. A little bit. But if you ask me, he knows about as much about girls as a rhino knows about fly fishing.

Kevin and Tyler are different. They are cool, really cool. They are like lonely wolves in the tundra, like knights who fall in love with their armor, which makes it kind of hard to notice the beauty all around them, especially flowers. When Kevin and Tyler see a field of flowers the only thing they see is whether it is a decent soccer field. Forget the flowers.

Diego the tornado is really serious and really funny. I've never met anyone who can think of so many funny things to say and do just to make life interesting.

His rule in life is to not take ourselves too seriously, and I really like and respect him.

Joey, too. He plays soccer as if he put a spell on the ball. He's a good friend already, even though he may not know it yet. I know it. I can see it in his eyes. I know I can rely on him completely.

That goes for Roger the hero too. His heart is too big for him, just like his eyes behind those coke bottle glasses. That's why he is such a braggart, and that's why he allows the neighborhood girls to torture him. Once a week he has to let those preschool stylists fuss over his hair.

But I think I can save him.

The only way to get rid of a curse is with a counter curse. Just imagine what'll happen when Roger and I grab those poodle-haired girls and explain the advantages of a David Beckham hairstyle.

Maybe it'll convince Roger that girls aren't really poisonous. Not all of us, anyway. And maybe I should have a word with Kyle's father, too, and ask why he wants to turn the best goalie in the world into a golf pro?

There are so many things I dream about, so many things I want to do in my life.

I would love to go on a secret outing with Julian Fort Knox. And I'm curious to hear what it's like to spend an entire evening discussing the U.S. Men's National Soccer Team with

Alex the cannon, the man with the strongest kick in the world, the man who is silent even on the phone. And I want to dance the samba with Fabio, the Brazilian soccer magician, and I want to sit on the grass with the *Wild Soccer Bunch,* sipping lemonade, and listening to Larry's stories.

Larry is the best coach in the world. I know he is. And if you ask me, the best coach in the world coaches the best team in the world.

I don't want to play with anyone else, and I'll tell you right here and now and forever; as long as the *Wild Soccer Bunch* exists, the U.S. National Soccer Team will have to wait.

JOACHIM MASANNEK
Joachim was born in 1960 and studied German and Philosophy in college. He also studied at the University of Film and Television and worked as a camera operator, set designer, and screenwriter in films and television.

His children's book series *The Wild Soccer Bunch* has been published in 28 countries. As the screenwriter and director of the five *The Wild Soccer Bunch* movies, Joachim has managed to bring about nine million viewers into the theatres. He was the coach of the real *Wild Bunch Soccer* team and the father of two of the players, Marlon (Tyler) and Leon (Kevin).

JAN BIRCK
Jan was born in 1963 and is an illustrator, animation artist, art director, and cartoonist. Jan designs the *Wild Soccer Bunch* merchandising with Joachim. Jan lives in Munich with his wife Mumi and his soccer-playing sons Timo and Finn.

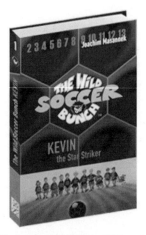

THE WILD SOCCER BUNCH
BOOK 1
KEVIN the Star Striker

When the last of the snow has finally melted, soccer season starts!

Kevin the Star Striker and the *Wild Soccer Bunch* rush to their field. They have found that Mickey the bulldozer and his gang, the *Unbeatables*, have taken over. Kevin and his friends challenge the *Unbeatables* to the biggest game of their lives.

Can the *Wild Soccer Bunch* defeat the *Unbeatables*, or will they lose their field of dreams forever? Can they do what no team has done before?

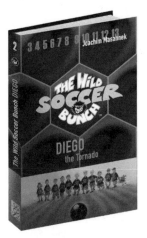

THE WILD SOCCER BUNCH
BOOK 2
DIEGO the Tornado

Fabio, the son of a famous Brazilian soccer player, wants
to join the *Wild Soccer Bunch*. But Fabio's father has other
plans. He makes his son play for the *Furies,* one of the best
youth club teams in the country. The *Wild Soccer Bunch* is
devastated, but Diego has a plan. He turns the *Wild Soccer
Bunch* into a club team and challenges the *Furies* to a
game! Can the *Wild Soccer Bunch* survive the game?
Can their friendship endure the test?

COMING SOON!

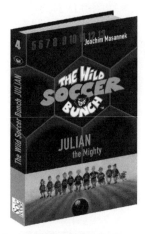

THE WILD SOCCER BUNCH
BOOK 4
JULIAN the Mighty

Julian Fort Knox, the All-In-One defender, is searching for his father who left one day and never returned. Along the way, Julian runs into Mickey the bulldozer and his gang and when they close in for the attack, the *Wild Soccer Bunch* is right there to help. One for all and all for one! The *Unbeatables* decide to challenge them to a rematch – an all-or-nothing "Match for Camelot." Sure, the *Wild Soccer Bunch* beat them once, but can they do it again?

The Wild Soccer Bunch
JUNIOR CHAMPIONS CLUB

Join the coolest club in the world!

Thank you for being a fan of the Wild Soccer Bunch!

You are invited to join our Junior Champions Club at:

www.wildsoccerbunch.com/jc

As a member of the Junior Champions Club, you get:

* The newest books in the series before everyone else!
* Rewards and prizes!
* Wild Soccer Bunch news and updates!
* And much more!

Love to read live to play!

Visit our web site for The Wild Soccer Bunch experience

www.wildsoccerbunch.com

Love to read, live to play!

Selected Reviews for Books 1 and 2:

"The Wild Soccer Bunch, book 1, is a mash-up of 'The Mighty Ducks' and 'The Seven Samurai' that every soccer mom will want on her child's reading list!"
—STEVEN E. DE SOUZA, SCREENWRITER, 48 HOURS, DIE HARD

"A soccer-centric, middle-grade series that's been making waves abroad is arriving in the U.S. There are now more than nine million copies of the books in print in 32 countries."
—PUBLISHER'S WEEKLY

"This book is a clear winner."
—AMANDA RICHARDS, TOP AMAZON REVIEWER

"A Great Read for Middle School Students! I am a middle school librarian and the students absolutely love the first book in the series "Kevin the Star Striker." There is nothing else like this series that I can find that is readable and appealing to the low and average middle school reader."
—C. THOMKA, SCHOOL LIBRARIAN

"A fun and exciting read for young soccer fans, *The Wild Soccer Bunch* is a top pick."
—MIDWEST BOOK REVIEW

"This is the kind of book that gets kids reading and begging their parents for the next book in the 13-book series."
—ROBIN LANDRY

"This is one of those books where you'll have a hard time putting it down; you will want to read the entire book once you start."
—Shawn's Sharings

"As a retired teacher, who has taught many reluctant readers, I highly recommend this inspiring book."
—Educationtipster

"A shorter read, which means that even reluctant readers will not be intimidated. The story moves at a quick pace... Great humor... wonderful illustrations. My picky 9-year old said he would read more in the series (this is huge!!!)."
—An Educator's Life

"If your child goes to bed wearing soccer cleats so they won't miss one minute of field time in the morning, he or she will fall in love with the *Wild Soccer Bunch*."
—JennyReviews.com

"This middle-grade novel isn't only fun and funny, it touches on some serious aspects of life."
—Imagination-Cafe Blog

"The writing is infectious and bodes well for a continuing series by this talented duo of Masannek and Brick."
—Grady Harp, Top Amazon reviewer

"*The Wild Soccer Bunch* is at it again and their humorously exciting antics will thrill the young reader."
—D. Fowler, Amazon top 50 reviewers, Vine Voice